Karl-Heinz Hermsch

The world without

METAPHYSICS

(A clear view of

human and the world)

(Revised edition)

Version: August 2025

1

Preliminary remark

There are, among others,

4 types, something consider.

(E.g. the content of a Non-fiction):

1. One cannot understand that.

2. You don't want to understand that because it doesn't fit your own worldview. *(So, not to the aims that created this.)*

3. You use your cognitive abilities to understand it.

4. One has judged beforehand and thinks one understands everything.

Prolog

In this book, the human being is viewed as a part of the universe. He, like everything in the cosmos, operates according to aims that are governed by laws.

The entire metaphysical, which used to play a major role because one wanted to explain everything with it out of ignorance, and some of which still has an effect today, are structures that have developed in the brain. If you take a closer look at them, you realize that they beyond that have no content.

There are neither non-material results nor experiences. Both take place in the brain - and this is material. This also applies to the spirit that is located in the neural networks (midpoints) or, based on an aim, is looking for possible ways to achieve it.

The hypothesis of a non-material was invented by metaphysicians to describe human states. At that time, the human brain was a mystery because the functions of the brain were unknown to them.

With metaphysics, mankind has not advanced a single step in knowledge for 2000 years. This way of seeing the world is a playground for some philosophers, who claim (without having to - or being able to) provide evidence - whatever comes to their mind.

Metaphysics calls itself a science. That's why she changed her name to ontology (especially the second syllable -logy is meant to indicate this). Whatever she calls herself; behind it is the claim that it creates knowledge. This is certainly not the case because everything she says is unverifiable. But it creates faith; self-felt belief.

Just saying: "What I believe and say is something spiritual, incomprehensible, which cannot be seen or proven" does not suffice as an alleged truth. Because with this statement everyone can justify all their fantasies.

Also, as an alternative to the ontology believers, I go the realistic way:

Everything that is written here below can be seen clearly and is provable.

In this book I summarize the basics of my findings.

The human psyche is shaped by his perception, which is influenced by the aims within him.

Awareness arises here, which can be defined as **increased attention to the sensory system**.

Man is controlled by midpoints. I use this term to describe neural networks that were created by aims.

The midpoint-mechanic is capable of influencing other neuron networks depending on the actuality; depending on what value they have for the current midpoints.

• In **aims**, I try to show that everything in the universe (including humans) is shaped by them.

• **Laws** always show an identical pattern when identical substances occur under identical circumstances.

• People like to speculate about the **universe**. Such as whether it is expanding or contracting. It should be clear that it is infinite.

• There is also a lot of speculation and fantasizing about **consciousness**. Although its task is only to cognitively enable people to recognize something better.

• In **perception**, I try to make it clear that we are not initially shown by the world as it is, but rather by the goals that are within us.

• With the **midpoint-mechanic**, I'm trying to make it clear that the neural networks of aims are developed to carry them out.

• **Life began about 3.5 billion years ago from matter - with the emergence of feelings and still judges based on them today.**

• **Artificial intelligence forms answers from facts.**

In the talks, "CP"
represents countless
discussion partners with
whom I have talk about the
topics for many years.

Contents

The central importance of aims

(Conversation about)

With the topic:

> Gestalt Psychology

> Universal scholar

> Consciousness Restriction

> Thinking habits

> Life Attitudes

> Fear of death

> Thirst for knowledge

If you want to know yourself, ask about your aims.

The most essential point is their nature: If they are not

**fulfilled, they urge,
depending on the
instantaneous or general
value in oneself with
feelings, to be somehow
achieved after all.**

"Aims (often synonymous with values) consist of networks of neurons and synapses, among other things. These act as knitting patterns and mark or generate a way to get there when activated. In this way they structure the brain and, in direct succession, people and the world. "

"You say that all living beings are aligned with aims. How did you come up to this? "*CP* was curious.

"I was wondering why people do what they do. And have repeatedly observed that aims (as midpoints) shape people - as long as they are in the waking state of attention. "

"And outside of wakefulness?"

"When you are asleep, or similar states where the midpoints have diminished in their activity, and the brain structure changes drastically. For example, the work of the frontal lobe is repurposed to a clearly limited extent.

The difference between wakefulness and sleep is that in the former the centers provide structure; the frontal lobe plays a significant part in the goals sought here. On the other hand, they are partially reduced to zero during sleep (the frontal lobe, such as the logical functions, are blocked). So, the midpoints have little influence on the brain, which can therefore conjure up the strangest images.

It is not uncommon for some excited emotions to be experienced unbridled as reality with lively fantasies.

So, other mechanisms and laws are active.

But of course, everything continues according to substances and laws - only according to other aims."

"How do you define aims?"

"Form a structure that leads to the desired endpoint of a path. For this, two things are needed: First, man must form a structure in himself and he must see the world in a structure that shows a suitable path. And that's how all living things do it, because their original goal is survival. "

"That means that the living being structures itself, takes itself into a different shape?" Asked CP.

"No, the respective aim is this form".

"Aims are very important in your theory building," stated CP.

"In fact, everything is structured," I nodded. "Take the system life. In every living being, there is a spectrum of aims that relativize, detach, connect with each other, form co-operative groups, cover up, wrestle for supremacy, and organize themselves into a partially alternate hierarchy. Aims are added, others change or go out. Each target has, or generates, its opponent, if other targets are touched and run the risk of being compromised. And every action takes place through a set of aims that each develop structures, compromise, reinforce or weaken. Many aims change in the course of life, except for the very low-lying, for example, the life instinct. This one always remains, even if you are very old."

"That sounds very complicated," said *CP*.

"It is, too," I nodded again. "The whole system is incredibly diverse and nested. That makes it so difficult to tell exactly where the driving forces of action come from.

Every behaviour, if traced back, will have its source in the life instinct. There are usually many intermediate stages between this and the current behaviour. That's why it's often hard to find the connections. But the younger a living being, the easier it is to determine. In the course of his life man differentiates more and more. It builds up more and more, depending on the aims it carries. "

"Can you never get to the bottom of the psyche?"

"Not in the smallest detail. But if you want to try to recognize yourself, it helps to know that everything is designed in one of midpoints - like the aims of the SELF, which are in the brain and play an important role.

Ultimately, people are always circling around the same aims, only the content is different. The ultimate aim is, as a rule, the life instinct, which, it seems, always wants to grow, wants more and higher, closely followed by the aim of orientation, showing man his environment, which is of value to him, in positive or negative Meaning, in order to be able to react accordingly. The most important design factor is then the group - starting with two people - the society in which one lives. The aim of being recognized is arguably one of the strongest in life. Thus, the society in which one lives can totally become one's own world, that is, it can express one's aims, in other words: Values that have been anchored in the socialization process can absolutely shape you and cannot lead to other aims in this regard."

"You say there's no life without a midpoint?"

"Let me redefine what I mean by 'midpoint': it means the world that is created to reach an aim. Everything else is more or less shielded. He selects from what he finds and believes he has a value for the aim, and gives shape to the world. Imagine the unimaginable: completely without aims. In you, the aim would no longer be to survive, to satisfy your needs, to orient oneself. From the very beginning of the first life in the world, you would find the aim of survival, which created the 'sight' and brought the found world into a form.

A strong aim can completely take over the human being for a period of time and structure it completely. This can be seen very well in the phenomenon of love, or when you have a task in front of you that completely engages you. Everything in one is aligned as much as possible."

"You meant the aims in man are hierarchical. Are you saying that there is a command center in the brain?"

"No, this is not existing. What I mean by this is that the more important the aims are, the higher the rank. To achieve this, neural networks join together to form jointly acting groups, ensembles. The hierarchy can change constantly according to the demands of the world."

"When and how did these networks actually come about?"

"Brain development in humans begins in the third week of pregnancy and is largely completed only after puberty, up to 20 years after birth.

The baby already has almost the entire amount of neurons at the time of birth, but only a small part of the neuron processes and synapses. These multiply after birth at a breathtaking pace and network the neurons, it forms a lot of networks.

These are then reinforced or dissolve again. "

"According to what rules?"

"According to the respective aims. It depends on what value they have in relation to the aims in the brain and how intensively they are used. The experiences with the environment determine which nerve networks become stronger, endure and which do not. "

"So, the decisive factor for this are the experiences that the living being has in the various phases?"

"The more important something is for a living being, the more it learns in this relationship. Neuronal networks are amplified, reshaped or re-formed."

"Do the individual neurons only react to a specific impulse?"

"No, they can form structures for different impulses with different neurons, they have a multiple function, so to speak: For the respective aims, many nerve cells have the possibility, in milliseconds, of an impulse with other cells, which have an equal potential in themselves to organize.

Take about a life-threatening situation. This structure over various activated neurons lightnings fast your shape. The more life, the survival is affected, the stronger the activities. "

"So, no order is given from 'above'?"

"The 'command' is the perception, the impulse, which is then translated into reactions - if there is an aim for it, and the impulse has the corresponding valence."

"What determines the valence?"

"The aims that lie in one."

"But if you say that the life instinct is usually at the top of the hierarchy, then it would have to be found somewhere!"

"It lies in the primordial structures of living beings that have passed it on through DNA."

"If one could define the aims in humans as associations of neurons, which u. a. are stimulated by stimuli to form a figure? "

"Yes. And in the same way that neurons can have multiple functions, so too are the individual aims: they can organize themselves into groups - into aims that can form action forms. At the same time, various aims are being stimulated in parallel, forming together forms. "

"Let me repeat: the impulse, the stimulus from outside or inside activates targets, these activate further neural networks and these again solution programs."

"That's the procedure," I confirmed.

"When you go from one midpoint to the other, is it like switching from one neural network to another?"

"Yes, the midpoint is made up of co-operating networks with their respective weights."

"Once again asked: Everything is subject to aims?"

"Yes, whether inorganic or organic."

"So not just the living beings?"

"Look: After the big bang there was mostly hydrogen, helium and some lithium and beryllium. From these gases galaxies with solar systems and planets developed under great pressures, and all the elements we know today formed during this time. All this was inorganic until a certain point in time. "

"And was shaped based on aims?"

"When substances or their environment are changed, different forms and laws result.

Everything has the aim of forming a figure according to the laws. Exactly that is also subject to everything organic. What they all have in common is that they are guided by aims. From this perspective, there is no difference between the inanimate and the animated. With the latter, 'only' the aims of survival are added, which have led to ever more complex structures.'

"Why do you often not see that aims shape you?"

"Quite simply because you believe you are shaping yourself with your consciousness."

--- Gestalt psychology ---

After a break, *CP* continued.

"You certainly know **Max Wertheimer**, who said: 'There are relationships in which not everything that happens as a whole derives from the way the individual pieces are and are composed, but conversely, where - in a pertinent case - what, what in a part of this whole happens, determined

23

by internal structural laws of this its whole. '"

I nodded. "These internal structural laws result from aims in man; they record for what he is receptive to, important to him, and save this as a wholeness. For example, listening to music is, of course, the melody and not the individual instruments. This holistic view is an important feature of all living things. "

"Wertheimer's Gestalt theory, then, seeks to clarify the laws by which the brain joins elements into a whole," concluded *CP*.

"These are explained neither by the laws of the individual parts nor by their sum," I added. "But they are explained by the respective aim in the human being, which brings all parts with its midpoint into a structure appropriate to the aim, which is then stored in the brain.

Holistic recognition makes sense to handle situations better and faster. "

"I'll summarize it again," said *CP*. "The holistic view of the brain has the aim of being able to make quick decisions - if it were to go into all the details every time, then this delays its capture or its decision. This holistic view arises in man through experiences that he has already made in similar situations. But since these are only similar, that does not necessarily mean that they are appropriate for an aim or that it correctly indicates a lying one. "

"Right. As a rule, this results in a figure that can be dealt with without losing himself in details. But it can also cause the brain to create something wrong. This can have unpleasant consequences, because you can live with these 'facts', which you can call suggestions, that influence attitude and behaviour. It is the cause of confusion of the most diverse kind. The creativity and imagination of the brain are limitless, it 'explains' everything. Especially if you do not know or recognize something. If you notice this and it is important, it corrects the aim."

"And you say everything in the universe is shaped by aims," *CP* was curious.

"Everything has the aim to form a figure according to the respective laws. Everything is aligned with aims. "

"Even a lifeless stone?" CP smiled.

"By 'lifeless stone' you probably mean something lying around somewhere. Well, I would like to say: First, there is movement within the stone, because it consists of atoms or even smaller particle waves, which are not motionless and also run according to laws. And secondly, when this stone is moved, then it forms with its environment, the circumstances of a particular structure according to the laws. That's what I mean when I say: everything has the aim of forming a figure according to the laws."

"Could a stone form a structure even without laws?"

"How come? This is impossible because the laws are inherent in the substances. Nothing can happen without laws, because the substances are laws! "

"And so, you came to the conclusion that everything has the aim of forming a figure according to the laws."

"Right, this happens completely automatically. It is not that a stone has a consciousness that is out to obtain information. He's not alive. But since, as I said, everything runs according to laws, the aim automatically arises to create structures according to the laws of nature.

The same thing happens to the living beings, except that here the aim of survival is added. This aim shapes the human being. This is what I call midpoint or midpoint-mechanics.

Imagine a person who has no more aims. So, do not eat anymore, drink, etc. What would happen to that? "

"He would probably die."

"By the way: without an aim, the placebo effect wouldn't work either.

The aim here is to achieve something through medication. This creates a midpoint that pulls in everything that is useful for that aim. Of course, also experiences that were made when you were already taking any medication that helped. The logic of the brain is: If a suitable drug, which comes from a competent person, is taken against this disease, then this aim will also be fulfilled.

As a result, the previous internal structure in this relationship can change up to the fulfilment of the aim: from illness to health."

"And this is done by the brain just because it "recognized" a drug that helps in his view?"

"Yes, that is enough. Unless, for example, the consciousness (better: the perception of the senses) gives the information that there is no active ingredient in the drug or that one does not trust the person who prescribed it. This would severely limit or negate the effect.

--- Consciousness restriction ---

The vast majority of human reactions are unaware. Consciousness becomes only a very small part, and always when something important occurs. Then information about the consciousness is obtained. If they are relevant, the brain processes them with the midpoints.

All other reactions and behaviours take place via the general, more or less strong, attention or automatically. "

(Senses attention; takes in the outside and inside world with the senses loosely - consciousness, i.e. increased attention, is specifically concerned with something.)

(Attention of the senses; takes in the outside and inside world with the senses loosely - consciousness of the senses, i.e. increased attention, is specifically concerned with some-thing.)

"But that must be an incredible amount of aims with their midpoints that shape the people!"

"Yes, you can say that. Just such a simple act as picking up a newspaper requires many learned aims that have been summarized and then run automatically.

Time and again, I hear that people have trouble understanding that everything is guided by aims, including themselves. I think its daily life that makes them fail to understand that sentence. Because everything is so natural, what happens. If they dig deeper, then they could see that every action, every movement is guided by aims and moves them. For example, the handle to the glass of water and drink from it. "

"Many people I've talked to actually have trouble understanding what 'aim' means," *CP* nodded. "For them, one aim is to complete a task or strive for something. But such a simple thing, such as bringing a spoon to your mouth, is not an aim for them!"

"Because it runs automatically, without paying more attention to this process. If they were to get to the bottom of this, they would come closer to the fact that every single hand movement must first be learned. The motivation for this was aims.

Because that's just the treachery for the realization that simple actions are taken for granted and not further think about it. Not realized that very specific aim-oriented processes are behind it."

"Yes, that's right," CP remarked thoughtfully.

"Lots of amazing achievements by people who are often based on island talents, for example to remember a large number of things in a limited time, to perform complex arithmetic operations in a few seconds or to learn a new language in a short time, would not be possible without an aim. This provides the structure that leads to the solution. Even artificial intelligence, which works with algorithms, does not come to a conclusion without a specified aim. "

--- thinking habits ---

I took a short break.

Then I continued: "Until the 16th century, people knew virtually no laws.

31

Everything was determined from God's perspective. But even in our time, many are far from seeing everything controlled by aims, thinking that most things happen by themselves anyway, and still viewing consciousness as something metaphysical or something. These views have passed from generation to generation and still shape some philosophers and people who deal with these issues. Everyone else usually just takes it that way because they do not even think about it. "

"Why don't man often see that aims shape him?"

"Simply because man believe that he shapes himself with his consciousness."

"What if they were to throw their antiquated views overboard and start thinking that consciousness is indeed just a brain information provider?"

"Most people are too caught up in their views, their habits of thinking. In the least, the aim is to get to the bottom of the processes in them, to deal intensively with

the course of their consciousness, as with this topic. Added to this there are innumerable people who live in the world of esoteric mysticism and, if they accept this insight, injure their world. For them consciousness is an essential element in the mystical view of the world, which is shaped by a metaphysical aim with its midpoint in them. "

"You mean they create this aim themself? "

"Secure. Without noticing it."

"The truth does not interest them, do you mean to say that," said *CP*.

"They are interested in the truth," I replied, "but only their truth". Everything else is labelled as nonsense.

One can call this the drama of the blinded human being. Its midpoint, the mystical world, surrounds it like a bell shielding all other views and evidence."

"Pity," regretted *CP*, "I find it always very exciting to hear and discuss new views."

"I feel the same way", I nodded. "Unfortunately, it is often the case that each of us has a world view that involves a more or less strong perseverance. Changes to beloved settings are reluctant to make.

For example, branded images and ideas of the culture in which you grew up are transported from generation to generation. Only too rarely are these questioned, and if so, often with bad feelings, because they question the structures they have created: in themselves and in society. Resistance quickly builds up, trying by all means to maintain the old structures. "

"Self-knowledge apparently does not belong to the aims of many people," said *CP*.

"I have that impression too. Self-knowledge comes through self-observation. Who does that?"

"Funny, I enjoy watching myself and sometimes have to laugh heartily when I've seen things wrong or insisted on an erroneous point of view. By introspection, one comes closer, sees moves in ones that have not yet noticed, especially in new or critical situations.

Maybe it's also because I can accept myself and my behaviour, with the sentence, 'What happened, had to happen as it happened.' "

"I feel the same way," I confirmed. "That's why I enjoy talking to you. I've learned a lot from you already. "

"The compliment I can give back, the discussions with you are very stimulating for me.

What aims should one have?", he continued.

"I can't answer that like that. The aim is to dictate something to others, not within me. Everyone has their own values. I can only speak for myself here, for my aims: The most important thing for me is knowledge. I can completely immerse myself in it.

What comes to mind is that dissatisfaction always depends on the level of expectation."

"You mean, the decisive factor is the respective goal?"

"The more you have achieved an aim, the higher the satisfaction - and vice versa. Here you can find roots for euphoria and especially depression.

Therefore, one should think carefully, which aims one undertakes. Are its wrong aims, for example, that cannot be achieved, then you open the door to bad mood or depression. False aims can severely burden the psyche. "

"Do you have ideals?"

--- life attitudes ---

"Not really, unless you count the truth."

"Would wealth and fame give you something?"

"If I had the sense of wealth, then I would have to write for the people according to their expectations. So,

36

fairy tales, sex, crime. These would not be desirable aims for me. I am absolutely satisfied with my life, in which I search for new insights. I have nothing of wealth, because what I want to know is primarily in me and rises spontaneously. So, much money would not help me in this respect.

And fame could possibly create vanity in me that does not help my actual aims, but rather hinders them. It could stop me from time to time questioning my theses and possibly insisting on them, even against legitimate objections.

There are enough examples of famous personalities. "

"You are different than most people."

"I did not aspire to that. I am the way I am, and that's how I take myself. "

"Why do people strive for greatness, for wanting to have more and more?"

"One reason will be vanity. An essential element of life is the recognition in the group, the society.

The general reasons will lie in the primordial structures. "

"Therefore, people are striving for wealth, build taller buildings, clothe themselves conspicuously, show what they have, try to achieve a high position in society?"

"I think that's the driving force. Many people are shaped by this. "

--- fear of death ---

"Are you afraid of death?"

"I know that the midpoint of life-drive creates this fear to drive people to continue living. For example, it does not matter to him whether human being is terminally ill and suffers from horrible pain or only wishes to die. Knowing the reason makes it easier for me to deal with these feelings. And: If you're dead, the reason is gone anyway, then feelings logically play no role anymore."

"Why do many people think that death is something very bad?"

"Because the life instinct is fooling everyone. He is the strongest midpoint of life. "

"But he is ultimately only an aim."

"Naturally. Therefore, for example, the suicide is also nothing wrong. Anyone who believes this merely reflects his own opinion or that of the society in which he grew up or lives. "

"And the own opinion is always relative," *CP* added.

"What do you think about near-death experiences?" He asked.

"Dying is the extinction of the organ functions of a living being, which leads to death. Death is the function setting of the neural networks in the brain.

Experiences can always only be gained through the brain. And as long as this is not dead, it is capable of producing fantasies. When the brain is dead, you do not experience anything anymore.

Near-death experiences come clearly from the brain. And the brain is not always right with what's coming out of it - that we see very clearly in the dreams."

So, one should not attach great importance to near-death experiences."

--- thirst for knowledge ---

"Can one say, Mr. Hermsch, you are always on the trail of yourself?"

"That's not quite true, but I often spontaneously have thoughts and feelings that I follow, with which I study intensively. I research, compare, falsify and verify and try, if they help me in my desire to understand, finally to bring them understandable on paper. Hoping to get criticized if I'm wrong about a view.

In addition, there is a strange striving for perfection in the relationship that I want to answer questions that are in me to the smallest detail. These aims are sustainable in me, so even if I have answered questions, they pop up again and again and make me check to see if my answer was correct or had any errors. "

"From uncertainty?"

"Out of openness and the pursuit of perfection."

"So, it's not just the urge for an answer that makes you think of something, it's the urge for it?"

"Through this quest for perfection fall to me answers. And since these aims are sustainable in me, there seems to be no end to it. That's why criticism is important to me. And that's why I write.

In addition, dealing with a question always raises new questions. So, my urge to learn never actually comes to a conclusion.

Even while falling asleep and sleeping, there are suddenly thoughts or ideas, for example, about topics that I had once occupied myself with, but where I had no solution.

I then take notes for a moment, because I had the experience that if I did not write it down right away, the thoughts would have disappeared the next day. A voluntary retrieval of these target solutions is not possible for me after I wake up again. "

"All this seems to give you a lot," presumed *CP*.

"I can be completely absorbed in it", I confirmed.

Laws are immanent and unchangeable.

(Conversation about)

With the topic:
> Causality
> Probability calculation
> Chaos
> Physical Laws and God?
> Meaning of life only through religion?
> Acceptance of nature
> Rules of good and evil

---

1. Identical substances under identical circumstances always give identical results.

2. The reason for this is that everything is subject to unchangeable laws.

3. If you change substances or circumstances, then other laws also appear.

That also means: There are no substances without laws.

No one can separate or change them. The formula: substances = laws is universal.

CP remarked: "Your definition of 'laws' is: Identical parts or waves in identical circumstances always result in identical structures."

I nodded.

"Is there something that is identical?" he asked sceptically.

"That's a good question. I have therefore formulated the sentence so that it is clear, well-defined.

As a rule, I express it in a modified form: the more similar substances and circumstances are, the more similar are the structures or laws resulting from them.

But back to your question: I would describe 'identical' like this: A substance - with or without mass - that matches all of its properties with another. It follows that both operate according to identical laws.

If 'identical substances under identical circumstances' did not achieve an identical result, then either the substances or the circumstances were not identical.

"Is there anything in the content of the universe that does not follow the law?"

"No, laws are inherent in everything.

That's why not everything is possible, only what the laws allow."

"You also claim that all laws are eternal," CP continued.

"That's right, the same substances in the same circumstances always result in the same thing. You can never change a law. However, as soon as you subtract or add something from a substance, other laws arise.

The Gestalt theory is suitable as an example. She says that the essence of something can only be grasped from its entirety, not if it is reduced to the individual pieces that make it up. The whole, which ultimately always creates the brain (and thus adds something), results in a new law and view of man."

"Where do the laws come from, who made them?" CP continued to research.

"Nobody did that, any more than anyone created the universe. As I said, they are inherent to the substances. "

There are no substances without laws.

"So, the laws are in the substances or the respective environment," CP thought out loud.

"Anyone can check that," I nodded. "The same things - or substances - in the same circumstances always result in the same thing. It is a universal law.

This is valid in the macro world as well as in the micro world, the world of the smallest particle waves. The only difference is that the micro-world is more susceptible to influences, such as interactions, and the laws here are more difficult to determine. "

"Why did only a few people notice that **everything** went according to the law?" CP asked thoughtfully.

"Because the world is constantly on the move. This movement incessantly creates new constellations, each of which runs according to different laws.

It would not be important for survival to realize that everything is done according to the law. It is important to react appropriately to changes. Therefore, there was no aim to check exactly whether the same substances always achieve the same result under the same circumstances - which is the definition of the law.

But anyone who tries to refute this sentence will conclude that it cannot be refuted."

--- causality ---

"What about the causality?", *CP* was still curious. "It says, that every effect has a cause."

"This is valid in the macro world as well as in the micro world, the world of quanta. In the macro world we live in, this is obvious if you look for the cause long enough.

In the microworld this is not immediately clear. Since it is much more difficult to measure or observe in the quantum world without interfering with the process, it is very often the case that coincidence occurs here. (I call coincidence ignorance of the legal process). Here, of course, causality is also present because the inherent laws of elementary parts and the local or non-local environment are the cause of the effects. That's how they build their structures. "

"So, the problem is not," concluded *CP*, "that in the quantum world, not everything works according to laws, but that one can observe and measure them much more difficult. So, you're dealing with a measurement or observation problem in general? "

"The word 'coincidence' is often used for this," I nodded. "Today, interaction-free quantum measurement can be used to measure very well.

Here comes a particular phrase that should not be forgotten: 'Everything has the aim of forming a structure according to the laws.' If you look for it, quantum mechanics loses the mystery and you take it for granted."

"How could one imagine elementary particles, such as an electron that is simultaneously wave and particle?" He was curious.

"Many elementary particles are subject to this fact. We are used to introducing ourselves to one or the other, for example in quick succession. Imagining a part in two exactly opposite properties at the same time is not possible for us, for example, to think of a cat as dead and alive at the same time.

An aid can be the yin and yang symbol. This is meant to express those opposing properties are one. When immersed in it, this image dissolves into a non-objective cloud. Such a cloud is also the reality of the elementary particles. "

"Atoms are made up of elementary particles, such as electrons, protons, neutrons, (and smaller elements, such as quarks, leptons, etc.), that is, virtual clouds," *CP* considered.

"Yes, atoms and their components are clouds, in which particles and wave form a unit. They run according to their inherent laws that determine when they fall apart.

That man cannot make predictions by observing or measuring the decay of an atom should be clear from what has just been said. Perhaps one can still imagine the virtual clouds, but then also recognizing the respective laws according to which they run is virtually impossible. "

"Well, just because we cannot make a precise prediction about the decay of an atom, and then conclude that something is happening out of nothing, has no basis whatsoever," concluded *CP*.

--- probability calculus ---

"That's clear," I agreed. "The particle-wave clouds are unimaginative to humans about the exact process. They are, as I said, neither exactly to measure nor to observe. Unless you try the math. Because this can make very accurate predictions with the probability calculus.

But that is only possible because everything is legal. And because the number of possible variations in a system is very diverse, but finite.

That's why not everything is possible.

Albert Einstein once said, 'How can mathematics, after all a product of human thought, regardless of experience, really match the realities?'

My Answer: Because the real thing is governed by laws. And because the particular set of structures involved in this relationship is limited.

This is to be understood, because mathematical probability calculus otherwise could make no clear statements.

"They say chaos, meaning complete disorder," *CP* commented. "You say, even in chaos, everything goes according to laws?"

"With the disorder, do you mean that predictions about the course are not possible?" I asked back.

"Yes," *CP* nodded.

"And when predictions are impossible, then disorder prevails?" I prodded.

"That's the way it is said."

"Well, in chaos move parts or particles, waves. Why should not this process be legal? "

"As I said, predictions about the course are not possible."

"It's the same knitting pattern as what we just discussed," I shook my head. "Because you cannot predict something, it is concluded that there are no laws, and we use the word coincidence. Is not that too easy? Because 'structure' can of course also mean 'disorder'. In this case, 'goal' simply means that processes are carried out according to laws and not that the parts form into a certain order according to the human imagination.

CP considered. "True," he said then, "it has yet to be proven. In fact, the chaotic behaviour we see is no proof that there are no laws here. "

I nodded. "Chaos also means the unpredictability due to the initial state of a system. For example, assuming two seemingly identical initial states, under the same circumstances, and the prediction of the result is different, then one has not included all the components that play a role in the initial state. "

"That would mean that everything is determined even in chaos, but not all components were known or taken into account," CP reflected.

"The opinion that not everything is done according to substances and laws, but is in this respect like fast. Out of ignorance and because we cannot dive into the chaos inside to see it closely. Not infrequently, to prove something mystical.

This scheme is used whenever it is difficult for a person to take a deeper look at what is happening. Like the dream, which often seems completely incomprehensible. "

"But it still runs according to the law?" CP assured himself again.

"For sure. Neurons work according to laws.

But you quickly reach its limits if you want to make concrete statements.

--- Physical laws and God? ---

How else than by law should the substances in the universe run out? "

"Well," replied *CP*, "there are people who say, by the hand of God."

"Well, can you imagine that, for example, physical laws can be changed by a hand movement of God or no longer apply?"

"Not really."

"People who say that are not serious in my view. They live in their world, in their midpoints and these simply exclude the facts, the reality with their complexes. Thus, man escapes reality."

"But they also argue: Can my feeling be wrong, that tells me with absolute certainty that God exists? Can my feelings tell me something wrong? "

"There is a clear answer to that: of course. If you look closely at his own behaviour, the question will answer itself. How often have people been deceived by their feelings?

By the way," I added, "laws like that did not exist before the seventeenth century. It was all destined for God by the people living then. "

"But after that," wondered *CP*, "it became more and more clear what role the laws play."

"Laws have the connotation of compulsion. People do not like compulsion. They prefer to believe that they decide to have their freedom. This is not conducive to the truth, but to their faith.

And then there are the cultural traditions that have carried on the belief in God from generation to generation. That was also gladly accepted, among other things, because it could temporarily escape the harsh reality. "

-- Meaning of life only through religion? --

"It is said religions are meaningful," *CP* interjected.

"Well, if you look at the history of religions, then you can conclude that they are nonsensical, to say the least moderately."

"But where should man get the meaning of his life? And what I always wanted to ask: what exactly does sense mean? "

"Gait, travel, walk, take a direction. So, meaning is the aim.

Regarding the question of the meaning of life: You can help other people, you can stand up for tolerance, you can lead a self-determined life for your most important aims, etc. In any case, these aims are laid out in people in their primordial structures. Mirror neurons, which I call mirror-midpoints, are activated. One sees or interprets the other, this stimulates similarities which again stimulate central points in one. This way one can feel similarly, empathize. You don't need a religion to react in a human way, for example to help.

If you look at what reasons the religions cite for their existence! And what religious beliefs have already done to other people's atrocities.

It is only people who have created the religions and who have then enforced other people according to their own, sometimes very selfish aims.

If one translates meaning with aim and looks at what religions have done, then one can only be warned against this 'meaningfulness'. "

"But what about the hold that faith gives people and from which they can draw strength?" added CP.

"That's another thing. This has nothing more to do with the external reality, but exclusively with the interior of man. There is no question that faith, as the midpoint, can help people to better face mental conflicts."

"But is not it too sober when you say everything is legal?" *CP* still came to mind.

"Since all substances are inseparable from laws, you should just take it that way. Look around the world at how colourful she is: people with their behaviours and ideas, nature in all its manifestations. Of course, everything works according to laws. Is that really only sober to call? "

--- Acceptance of nature ---

"I remember," *CP* changed the subject, "is the fact that everything works according to laws, for the people, for the society to accept at all?"

"That's a good question. You could have asked: Do people like the bare truth? "

"So, the truth you're standing for," *CP* noted.

"Everyone has the opportunity to refute my truth or to find one's own.

I believe, following my truth, that one would then stand between the acceptance of reality and its own midpoints. For the aims in man, in society, of course, want to be realized. This is the truth in the way and it is probably rather ignored, because otherwise the aims would seem to be impossible to achieve.

For example, if someone stole something, it is understandable from the point of view that everything had to happen the way it did, but it does not fit with the values, aims of the people who demand punishment and retribution. "

"How could one unite these fundamental opposites?"

"Through tolerance and insight, on the one hand, saying it had to happen that way, and on the other hand, our rules are important to us. You could argue, "If you get off scot-free now, our rules would be in jeopardy. And more importantly, this would apply not just to this case, but eventually over time. That could lead to internal tensions in society.

This tension can only be resolved by judging, 'You have broken a rule that applies to all of us, including you, and that is why you must be punished.

It's true that everything had to happen the way it did, but a society would break apart if you accepted everything and let everything go. Because it is held together by rules. "

--- Rules of good and evil ---

"Where do these rules come from?"

"The ideas of good and evil are formed unconsciously or consciously, unwritten or written, for example through the primordial structures in the human being, a cultural imprint, as aims in each group or society. These assessments then act more or less in the form of social norms and moral concepts in every member of society. "

"You mean," summed up *CP*, "who did something that harmed others, and believes he does not have to take responsibility for it, because: what had to happen, how it happened, should be remembered has violated the rules or laws of a group or society that would not be viable in the long run without them.

Because the opinion that others represent, their judgment, of course had to be done as it happened. Therefore, the offender cannot blame the judges for the verdict.

With the sentence: 'Everything's going according to laws', it should only be shown that everything had to happen the way it happened. "

"You have reproduced that well," I agreed.

"So, as far as possible, elements of understanding should be taken into account when assessing the sentence and should be included in the judgment," added *CP*.

"Yes, but most people will hardly worry about it because they just want to stay in their midpoints, and such insights are obstacles. So, they will have little understanding of the wrongdoing of other people (wrongdoing in terms of the aims of society). "

"But a big plus to the attitude that everything is predetermined," stated *CP*, "is that you can come to terms with what happened in the past more quickly."

"That's true," I agreed. "It's even a huge gain, because it makes you live more in the present and is less shaped by the past.

For example, the anger that breaks out in some people when they have not reached their goal is not very meaningful in view of what we have just discussed.

This is especially true for mistakes we make. So, if we curse ourselves, it can be particularly destabilizing for one's self. "

"But humanly understandable," he interjected.

"You're right.

Another advantage of the attitude that everything had to happen as it was is the tolerance that comes from the sentence and can have a positive effect on yourself and living together with other people.

One more word about the punishments that people pronounce against others: A deed is usually judged by the degree to which one was hurt in one's feelings. These feelings, it is demanded, should also be compensated by the judges by punishment. "

The **universe**

(Introduction)

> The universe didn't come into being - it was always there: Nothing can come from nothing!

> *Wikipedia: "The universe (from the Latin universus 'total'), also called the cosmos or the universe, is the totality of space, time and all matter and energy in it."*

Most people mean by the universe the observable; this is limited to the matter and energy found, starting with the elementary particles up to the large-scale structures such as galaxies and galaxy clusters.

And they usually assume that the Big Bang is the beginning of the universe.

This means that here **the joint <u>emergence</u> of matter, space and time took place from a singular point - which developed from nothing.** This then suddenly expanded with unimaginable speed.

What came before, or where this came from, is often answered by experts with 'nothing'. They don't want to admit their ignorance.

Here we are talking about a space that man has limited with his limited view.

(He saw and likes to see himself as the centre of the world.)

The beginning of the singular point cannot be proved; Even the general theory of relativity responsible for this, together with the quantum field theory, cannot describe this in a uniformly clear manner.

So, a cognitive being can assume that there was something before that that gave rise to the Big Bang.

To the big bang

This was invented by the Belgian Georges Edouard Lemaître (1894 - 1966). He describes the structure as a huge primordial atom, a kind of cosmic egg and claims that there was absolutely nothing before it; So, neither a universe, nor matter, etc. His followers then took over that.

Since he was also a priest in his life, the suspicion is very close that the reason for his statement that "the Big Bang came out of nothing" should actually mean: from God. Since he would make himself more unbelievable by doing so, he probably preferred to keep this as secret.

As I say: I think nothing can come out of nothing. And so, I argue further, an extreme gravitational accumulation of matter in the universe probably led to the event that gave birth to **our cosmos**.

I continue to think that such events occur again and again in the infinite, timeless universe.

So, a phenomenon in the universe could be **that everything can contract in one area**. In a critical state, which occurs when nothing more can be absorbed, everything flies apart in a gaseous state.

Therefore, I continue to assume an infinite universe **whose space has no limits and contains much more than that contained in the "singular point".**

The universe

(Conversation about)

With the topic:

> Own world page
> Big Bang page
> Omnipotence page
> Origin of belief in God page
> Brain processes page

"Your postulate is that there is only one universe, this is limitless and eternal," said *CP*.

"Not that I'm misunderstood," I replied. "It's not about the content here, but about the space of the universe - which is limitless and contains everything, including the state of empty spaces."

"Limitless, therefore," asked GP, "because a limit always entails the question: And what is behind this limit?"

"There is no limit to the universe."

"And forever, because there are no other spaces, time, or energy that can replace or change the universe?"

"It's all included."

"Why should one differentiate between space and content?"

"Because the space is infinite, the content - since this cannot be multiplied in the universe as a whole and already contains everything - is finite.

Both are eternal, only the content is, depending on the natural laws, 'infinitely' variable, constantly changing the structure.

Therefore, statements like: 'the thing in itself' or 'eternal ideas' in the universe also make no sense. There is nothing fixed, immutable.

The reason for this comes from the psychological structure of the person who says something like that. The aim here is the feeling in the brain that projects faith and this worldview.

The 'thing in itself' should be intelligible, that is, it should be able to be grasped spiritually by humans. It is the wish to have expressed something in the end 'originally finite'.

The 'thing-in-itself' should be intelligible, abstract, only mentally comprehensible by humans. It stems from the desire to have expressed something ultimately 'originally finite'.

It should therefore only be recognizable by the intellect, not perceptible to the senses.

Intelligible means that it can only be grasped spiritually. This usually means a metaphysical spirit that exists beyond the concrete world and works in people.

I think that this is a dream, born from the aim that there might be such a thing.

There is, of course, man's spirit, i.e. his cognitive abilities. But this is tied to his psyche and its midpoints; so physically. And here all kinds of speculations can arise.

"Eternal ideas" have people in the primordial structures - this is projected onto the outside world as 'objective metaphysical reality'. "

"But back to the universe: Constructs are constantly being invented to show how the universe came about," I regretted.

"One should realize that one does not speak about the universe, but about its content or parts of the (human) Worldview."

"How is that?" he asked. "Why do not people distinguish this?"

The reason will lie in the human experience, in the brain: everything has emerged from something. This is transferred to the universe. But neither the universe nor the entire content (as primordial substances) had a beginning.

"Of which one could say: 'That's where it came from?'" "

"Exactly. Because there was no beginning. And out of nothing, nothing can come. From this it follows that the substances have always been present in the content of the universe.

People say that everything has a reason, e.g., that there is a first mover who initiated everything.

Such a 'mover' is not necessary because everything runs according to substances and laws that are inextricably linked with one another. The substances can of course move on their own due to the laws within them. So, there is no need for a first mover, because the reason for movement lies in the substances themselves or in the environment. And, as I said, these substances did not have a beginning, did not arise, but have always been there in the universe (as primordial substances). "

"How do you define 'substances' and 'laws'?" *CP* asked.

"'Substances' are elementary particles, structures, atoms, neutrinos, molecules, neurons, crystals, liquids, gases, cells, living things, brains, forces, facts, things, living things, ideas, ecosystems, stars, star systems, galaxies, etc.", he answered. "In addition, they are also considered as virtual substances in states of empty spaces (the vacuum in space)."

"So, everything?"

"Yes," I nodded, "invariably. Everything in the content of the universe is considered a substance: on a large scale, like galaxies - which are relatively tiny in relation to infinity - or on a small scale like elementary particles. And of course, everything in humans.

'Law' means that identical parts - or waves - always give identical structures under identical circumstances.

Laws are properties of substances that, viewed in isolation, are unchangeable unless something is added to or removed from the substances.

And that means that everything can only proceed in a very specific form."

"Substances and laws belong directly and inseparably together?" *CP* suggested.

I nodded. "Yes, there are no substances without laws, you cannot separate or change them. The formula: substances = laws is universal. "

"Could you call it a world formula?" *CP* asked.

I considered. "In the sense that it applies to the entire world? That would be an option.

Adding to or subtracting from identical substances produces others that are subject to this formula. This can be seen very well in chemistry."

"You mean: if something is added to the identical substance or if it becomes less, then a new substance with different laws results. The substances therefore each run according to the laws inherent in them."

"That's the same," I nodded. "Everything is going according to laws. In addition, everything organic runs in addition to the laws of midpoint-mechanics. "

--- Own world ---

"To come back to the word 'world' again," *CP* remarked, "you also say everyone lives in his own world."

"There you should distinguish between the entire world - the content of the universe - and our views of it.

It's the midpoint-mechanics that make it possible for everyone to live in their own worlds: the midpoints, by their aims, bring man and the world into a structure that excludes everything else that does not suit them. Since ultimately everyone in his aims, which are midpoints, different from other people, everyone also lives in his own world. However, the more similar aims are with other people, the more similar are their worlds. This can also be seen very well in groups whose goals are more and more similar to, usually unconscious compromises, and thus create a corresponding world. "

--- Big Bang ---

"I would like to come back to the Big Bang, which is seen by many as the beginning of the universe," GP said. "If you ask where that came from, what was there, then it is said that everything was created from contracted energy - as a singular point. If you keep asking, you usually won't get an answer.

Or said; it came out of nowhere. I.e., it is claimed that the Big Bang did not come from the universe but created it itself," I said.

"Since people like to explain everything; the big bang theory comes in very handy; that would give him the very beginning of the universe."

76

GP nodded thoughtfully, "but can't it be that a content of the universe has actually united at this point? That it was just a change of state in a larger area of the universe?"

"You're probably right about that. So, would settle the question of the origin of the singular point."

We were silent. After a while I continued: "But maybe it's on purpose. Since the inventor of this theory was also a priest during his lifetime, the suspicion is very high that the reason for his statement that 'the Big Bang came out of nothing' should actually be: from God. But since that would make him less credible, he probably preferred to keep it a secret."

"And if you put it like you did?" GP thought about it. "**Our world** began with the Big Bang."

"That would probably be a valid statement and one that would be difficult to refute," I replied. "Many speak of the Big Bang, the beginning of the universe, or that the universe expands or contracts, etc. From the standpoint that there is only one universe, infinite and eternal, all these statements are pointless. They only make sense when you say, 'the beginning of **our** world' or **'our world** expands'. But since these formulations are only human perspectives, but humans want to give universal answers, one will probably continue to use the term 'universe', although this is not appropriate for these statements. "

"Because people think they have expressed everything with it?"

"I think it only creates confusion about the truth."

"And - do you believe that people, when they realize that, will change their idiom?"

--- Omnipotence ---

"Well, in this content of the universe, God would no longer have room with his alleged omnipotence. Because everything consists of substances that run according to laws and God does not have the power to change them. "

"So, because people could not live out their divine fantasies then?"

"I think that will be an important reason. Topics like Universe or God allow for all sorts of fantasies. People love fairy tales.

But anyway, no matter what facts you say, there fantasies will continue to live. "

"Believers say that God is the universe, limitless and eternal."

"Could he, in his omnipotence, change laws? The definition of laws is: Identical parts - or waves - under identical circumstances always result in identical structures. "

"They would say that he could too."

"Could he then change the universe, in this sense himself? Does not he also abstain from substances and laws like everything in the universe? Has one ever seen - and is it scientifically proven - that an almighty God has repealed laws? He would have had enough of the cruelty that happens on our planet every day. "

"You are right."

"That's what I meant when I said that the fantasy product 'God' with its alleged omnipotence has no place in the universe. And - if God is the universe, these people express at the same time that God consists of substances that run according to laws."

"Others say God created the universe."

"Then God would create a universe where everything has to be done exactly as it happens."

"And in which there is no freedom!", *CP* concluded.

I nodded. "Because you cannot change laws.

Here I would like to quote Max Planck: 'The truth never triumphs; its opponents only die out.'

Ideological concepts, such as religions - for example: there is a God, absolute freedom or a free will - stand the knowledge, the truth in the way. They are midpoints that do not allow that there is no God or ultimately no freedom.

It is impossible for these people to know the truth because they assume false assumptions. They see what they want to see (from the point of view of their aims)."

"Here, reason, intellect, intelligence hardly have a chance?"

"Absolutely none. Obstacles in the form of confusions and emotions trickle away everything. "

"Where do these obstacles come from?"

--- Origin of the belief in God ---

"The concept of the head, the leader you trust, has a subordinate part to it. This was particularly important for living beings, like the primitive people, in order to have aims, such as role models, in order to survive best Original structures established and is the actual cause from which the term "God" was formed.

And then, among other things, from the development processes of childhood, from the 'magical phase': This begins around the age of three and lasts for about two to three years. Between the age of three and five, she influences the child's thoughts and actions. In particular, the primordial structures in the brain probably play a role here. During this period, anything is possible in the childish imagination. Everything that the child desires and thinks, beautiful as well as terrible, could actually happen. What it thinks and does it see as an important cause of much that happens. At the same time, the child fears that other children and adults, but also witches, fairies and monsters could do something similar in the same way. Things and events are largely magically experienced by the child, and 'magical theories' try to interpret and explain them. Witches, monsters and ghosts, but also Santa Claus, Christ Child and Easter Bunny really do exist in the childish conception. '"

I continued, "Pretty much all of us humans go through this magical phase, and in each of us it lives on more or less until the end of life. Because experiences that we once felt to be important often remain emotionally intact for the rest of our lives.

This phase will be one of the main reasons why fairy tales, myths and sagas have a strong appeal and why God, for example, is considered a real being. And these fantasy templates are then further developed in the culture and with the views that prevail in society."

"Can the magic phase explain why many adults still believe that everything is possible? Even though it's not possible to change laws?"

"Yes, this should have a significant impact on adult thinking. Some still believe in mystical figures inside, such as gods, fairies, the devil. This is where superstition has its roots."

"So, magic and religion have their origins first in the primordial structures and then mainly in the magical phase," *CP* concluded.

"But people do not want to recognize, but project into the outside world.

Ones again:

> **The concept of the chief, the leader, whom one trusts, has an essential part in the original structures. This was particularly important for living beings, such as prehistoric people, in order to have targets, such as role models, in order to best survive.**
>
> **It is very likely that the actual cause from which the term "God" was formed can be found here.**
>
> **Since this is deeply anchored in the nature of people, he is also shaped in the present by the aim of submitting to someone, especially through feelings.**

By the way: All phases, especially those that the child goes through up to around the age of seven, form feelings that can be of decisive importance in later life.

For example, the attachment behaviour: through the physical contacts, usually with the mother, strong positive feelings of the people and the world, which are stored in the infant or toddler and remain lifelong. The people would like to experience these feelings in their further development and adulthood and therefore seek closeness and contact with other people. "

"Often one hears the sentence: I have the feeling, God loves me," *CP* still remembered.

"Cannot it be a transmission of the feeling of being loved by the parents, especially in childhood?" I asked.

CP looked pensive. "You may be right."

--- Brain processes ---

After a pause I said, "But in fact everything is possible - in the brain. This can be seen, for example, in fairy tales that are believed to be true, to the fantasies of believers or what you perceive in your sleep. "

I nodded. "The brain is already doing strange things, especially in sleep."

"Because much that matters in the daily routine is degraded during sleep," I added. "The attention or consciousness does not send information to the brain; the midpoints are shut down while sleeping."

"They do not play the role then as in the waking state?"

"This cannot work because sleep would be disturbed by the midpoints.

Or vice versa: Imagine your brain acting like it is in sleep during the day."

"You mean, if the aims, the midpoints, which are active in the course of the day, no longer determine the course?"

"One catastrophe would follow the other. That's why they put the brain in a certain structure whose main aim is survival.

In sleep we do not need the goals of survival in this value. Unless something extraordinary happens. Then, of course, we'll be wide awake immediately, and the usual midpoints will take over the direction again.

The difference between being awake and being asleep is, among other things, that in the former the midpoints provide a certain structure, whereas in sleep they are partially reduced to zero. **For example, in areas of the frontal lobe that are being repurposed.** So, they have little influence on the brain, which can therefore conjure up the strangest images through associations, connections and goals without a midpoint-mechanism."

"When you're awake, it's mostly about goals - when you're asleep, it's about themes," GP concluded.

"Yes. However: If a midpoint occupies a person in general, then this topic can also occupy him in his sleep-in order to find a solution.

"When awake or asleep, the brain acts like similarities," *CP* repeated. "The difference between the states lies in the aims.

While the brain serves the aims of the midpoints of the day when it is awake, i.e. it searches for what fits the midpoints so that they can reach their goal, these are usually almost inactive when we are asleep. Themes play the roles here."

"Exactly," I nodded. "The dream spins out of a story another story, etc. Reality, as we know, does not matter. But one should not forget: in the dream, the sentence: 'Everything has the goal to form a structure according to the laws', not abolished. Neurons = laws. "

"Then it just runs according to other laws!"

I nodded again. "By other compounds of the substances. Also, regarding the aims of relaxation and integration of the experience during the day. They relativize the information of being awake.

And as I said: In the dream, the day midpoints lose their power, and are subject especially to the laws of creativity. "

"The dream is so difficult to understand when you are awake," concluded GP, "because you are then back in the usual midpoints. Whereas in the dream these midpoints are dissolved and only possibly act as themes. This ends immediately when we awaken and the areas of the frontal lobe are again structured by the midpoints."

"Because the dream then usually has no value, is not important for the present," I underlined. "In sleep, associations, largely uninfluenced by the awake midpoints, can play their game."

Then I went on to say, "You can imagine the brain as a huge space filled with neurons, synapses, myelin sheaths, glial cells, dendrites, and axons that form nets."

"By that you mean the midpoints of the brain that run according to the laws in them."

"Exactly, there are endless possibilities for variation among each other, especially when strong midpoints, as in sleep, hardly play a role. The brain can in the dream among other things use all the experiences that man has made and weave them into bizarre webs. By the way: if it has not made certain experience, like a blind child, it will not use any pictures. "

"The brain works and processes in dreams," GP concluded.

"Yes, but not from a logical point of view. Dreaming means, among other things, being creative. However: The more rigid the midpoints are, and this particularly affects the complexes, i.e. encapsulated midpoints, the less they can be worked on in the dream."

"By 'complex' you mean an area in the human being that is inaccessible."

"Yes, he eludes change through other midpoints. He remains unaffected by the change in external circumstances.

The complex still shows the behaviour and feeling as it had in the original situation.

Since the central point of life is adaptation, all psychic aims should be adaptable, changeable, with their midpoints. Complexes resist any kind of change, but affect other midpoints. But anything that is rigid can be an obstacle to the flexibility of the psyche."

"Finally, I have one more fundamental question: You say: 'Identical substances under identical circumstances always give an identical result.'"

I nodded.

"But can't it be that somewhere in the infinite universe this sentence is not true?"

"Well - I don't think so. But of course, I let myself be taught better. If someone proves that to me through an experiment."

Consciousness

(Conversation about)

With the topic:

"You say Consciousness is an amplification of the senses," summarized CP. "And you mean it doesn't make any decisions."

"Consciousness is enhanced sensory awareness (taking in environmental stimuli and bodily states and relaying them) using a voluntary or involuntary focus to provide the most accurate information possible to targets in the brain," I nodded.

"That's a description that most people are probably unfamiliar with."

"Because they project into 'consciousness' the entire 'freedom of human beings' without examining them in detail."

"You mean, it would ultimately come out that it's just an information transmitter for the brain?" asked CP.

▶ "Consciousness (the heightened senses) or normal attention might not interpret the world sufficiently for decision-making because that is the domain of the brain; it neither possesses its information nor can it experience it at the necessary speed to react.
▶ The brain needs the information from consciousness (the senses) in order to possibly correct its interpretation of the world and to decide differently or to change its aims.

> **"Before we think we've made a decision, the brain has already made it milliseconds beforehand - when, as a rule, consciousness is no longer**

It is important to know: life always also means: experiencing feelings. And that the brain is their memory, in the respective neural networks. "

"But why do you need consciousness at all, because the information from the senses could also be stored in the brain without it?"

"That is also done with normal attention. But if something is important and essential, you have to look at it more closely. This is the job of consciousness.

Feelings in particular are eminently important because they are of outstanding importance for people with regard to aims.

As I said: the brain does not perceive. It just builds the world for us according to its aims. In other words, it takes its attention or consciousness from this perspective, experiences it with this "reality" that is then present and transfers the information to the brain.

That is why we must have attention and, in reinforcement, consciousness. "

▶ **"The world as a whole, in all parts, is not as we see it, but always like our brain, to be more precise; his aims they show us", recapitulated CP.**

"Many people don't realize this," I nodded. "For them, the world is as they themselves and others (apparently also) see: the same and unambiguous.

The fact that aims in the brain shape the respective world according to our dispositions and experiences, which only human perspectives can evoke, is usually strange and unimaginable to them. So, they ignore it, stick to their old point of view. "

"So, we cannot see the world objectively*."

"Always from our subjective perspective."

> **!! The world that shows itself to us is there first, but what a person sees of it, the brain decides according to its aims. !!**

Since what is important is always conscious in order to look at and experience it more closely, consciousness is always included.

It can only be this, however, if the midpoint in which one is currently does not devalue what is important through its aim.
(See midpoint-mechanics)

It is not uncommon for there to be differences between midpoints about what is 'important'. Especially with the SELF. What this desire can be blocked by other midpoints.

In other words, what a person perceives is decided by the aims in the brain - including what is important at the moment.

From this it follows: The senses (i.e., the consciousness) do not absorb it at all, because no aims are receptive to it, since the strong midpoint in which one is currently has temporarily reduced the value of them.

CP's eyes shone. " I understand that information is not recorded because the brain is not receiving it at the moment - not an aim - because the current network of neurons blocks all others."

I nodded. "If it were still necessary to prove that the consciousness is neither free nor can it make decisions, it is obvious here."

"There is another obstacle to understanding in the form that it is often claimed that the inorganic, i.e., matter, cannot produce anything organic.

I would like to say: The first organic compounds arose from inorganic substances billions of years ago. Over time, more and more complex and more complex forms of life with differentiated functions developed from this, including the brain.

Here are not only atoms, etc., but in particular also neurons, synapses, and so on, which control the physical and mental functions of humans.

The adaptation pressure of life generates aims. The brain forms neural networks to execute them.

Many people cannot imagine that only aims in the brain control people. They believe they control themselves (with their free will and consciousness). They cannot prove this, so it remains with a feeling that it is so and has settled.

So, they cannot perceive that in this case, the aim of their faith (this midpoint) causes it.

And: Not only the perceptions are stored, but, as I said, the resulting feelings. The stronger they are, the more intensively we have experienced them with our consciousness. "

"Consciousness is experienced, the brain reacts, controls and decides," recapitulated CP.

I nodded. "The brain shows us the world on the basis of its aims - the consciousness initially sees it from these. In the second step, however, it also experiences the possible differences between the old one from the brain and the new one, which it is now also picking up - and sends this information to the brain."

"Then, following your argumentation, the world that we see afterwards would also have to change, if it has a corresponding value."

"That's exactly how it is; we perceive it differently now.

We usually do not notice this because these changes are natural and logical for the brain. "

Let me briefly outline the process:

- The brain shows us the world according to its aims.
- Consciousness sees them in this form plus that which the senses then additionally absorb.
- It sends this information to the brain.
- This then shows us the world that may have changed due to the information.
- The consciousness then sees them in this form plus that which the senses now also absorb.
- It sends this information back to the brain.

These sequences repeat themselves constantly - in fractions of milliseconds. Depending on the value, with normal attention or with reinforced senses (consciousness).

This can be verified in experiments: What you see is initially only done by the brain. Then we experience it with our senses. This is sent to the brain which processes it. And then, depending on the deviation, shows the attention a corrected view.

Consciousness or normal attention cannot interpret the world because it does not possess all the information of the brain. This cannot experience, it needs this information of the consciousness in order to possibly correct its interpretation of the world."

"Is that the same when someone wakes up in a completely unfamiliar environment?"

"Yes. But the perception of the senses works very quickly - and sends it to the brain so that, when it is important, it adjusts in a flash, accepts this view and takes it into account when making decisions.

The central point of all living things is the preservation of life. This works best by **experiencing** it.

And these, in turn, are important information for the brain that couples and stores it with each event. Without consciousness, one could not experience this because, as I said, the brain alone cannot.

If a similar situation occurs, then the corresponding feelings are activated again.

(The danger here is, if one does not consciously perceive the current situation, that one reacts not to the now, but to the past.)

"It's about attention," CP considered.

I nodded. "Attention" means being at work. 'Consciousness' means to intensify your attention. The latter usually occurs much less.

In any case, the consciousness would not be able to conclude judgment without the brain, because the set of factors for it is much too large and variable to make decisions regarding the necessary activities and actions. It would simply be overwhelmed.

It would have to generate and control processes that are constantly taking place in the brain. "

"That would hardly be possible," agreed CP.

"But", he interjected, "it is sometimes objected that when you operate a machine, you don't have to know its functions down to the last detail. It is enough to press the right buttons. "

"Consciousness would have a lot to do there and should know **which actions** in the brain are to be activated in each case.

The brain is neither a device nor a machine, nor is it a computer. All of these comparisons are lagging because brains don't work as rigidly as those just mentioned.

The brain is a structure that organizes itself through its aims. In other words, a fabric that works according to organic laws and can change its value at lightning speed if the adaptation makes it necessary.

Therefore, these objections make no sense! They are just not properly thought out.

Its follows", I continued: "The brain judges. What <u>one</u> takes in by means of the senses can, depending on the value, eventually influence the decision. Because all information can have an impact on the brain – as long as it is open and flexible* – i.e., not blocked by rigid settings or a particularly strong midpoint at the moment.

However, the brain decides to what extent they reach according to its aims.

The better one knows its functions, values and possibilities, the more influence one may have with one's SELF and the will (which is also in the brain)."

"So, 'know yourself'?"

"Know your aims, so your psyche*.

Whoever observes himself, when he consciously picks up something, will find that his senses are strongly activated. Much stronger than if it's just about general attention.

You take in life with your senses, and when something special happens, e.g., something interesting, dangerous, emotionally moving, then you also take it up intensely with your consciousness, i.e., with heightened senses.

If people are dealing with a special topic, then they need specific information."

"The aim formed in each case may concentrate on the topic, and the consciousness (i.e., the increased perception) thus provides the brain with more precise facts," concluded CP.

"Thinking, for example," I explained.

CP raised his hand. "May I intervene briefly?"

I nodded to him.

"How do you define 'thinking?'"

"Thinking is a process that seeks to answer questions in the midpoints, i.e. neural networks. – Everything that man has inherited and experienced can be found here.

This creates the loop: question>answer>question again>answer, etc.

Based on a stimulus or a question, the senses look for information in the outside or inside world and immediately send it to the brain. This looks for experiences or similarities. You become aware of these interim results again, etc. The interplay goes on until you have a coherent feeling or you can't get any further. The end product of thinking is formulated by the brain and only becomes conscious for a fraction of a second or later. "

CP considered. "What comes out, is so decided or formulated by the brain?"

"Yes, by the aim's neural network formed for this quest, making the final decision. And excludes all other non-relevant neural networks.

The reason that people believe that they have made their decision based on their consciousness lies in the very short period of time - often, as I said, it is only milliseconds - between the decision of the brain and becoming conscious (i.e., taking in with the senses).

When it comes to important issues, there is always an interplay between the brain and consciousness, because the brain has only a limited amount of current information and relies on the consciousness, as an amplifier of the senses, to add new facts if necessary."

"Only the most important things become so conscious?"

"Yes".

"Who decides what is important?"

"The aims with their midpoints."

"There are many people who claim that you decide everything with your consciousness," CP came back to this topic.

"It's incredible what it's supposed to mean," I said. "Once you look through the definitions, you read: knowing certain facts, remembering certain events, sum of beliefs and points of view, etc.

And synonymous words for consciousness should be: intelligence, memory, conviction.

The consciousness should also have complete access to the brain, "read out" the relevant data there and evaluate this data in order to be able to make a decision. After the decision, he would have to intervene again in the neural networks of the brain, for

107

example to start movements that are necessary to carry out the action he has chosen.

All of this applies exactly to the brain. But once you check the consciousness what it represents of it, you search in vain. Because it was not made to carry this around with you and it cannot do it at all. "

"So, people say that they control themselves with their consciousness, because they are not observing themselves closely, because they take these views for granted. They just parrot out of habit what other people say or what they have learned. This also includes using the word consciousness without reflection. "

"That hits the nail on the head," I confirmed.

"They just take it that way."

"Yes, because they have either not yet heard the statement that man is a being guided by aims of the brain or they do not want to hear it. It interferes with their usual views of the world they want to stay in. Accordingly, they do not investigate this matter either. "

"Does that also apply to scientists?"

"Unfortunately, yes. Their feelings do not let you see these facts."

"Does that come from the midpoint-mechanics?"

"Yes. They are at the midpoint of their feelings.

These also generate the opinion that consciousness is something that only humans have and that they control themselves with it.

--- Expansion of consciousness ---

By the way: The expression 'expansion of consciousness' also comes from this attitude. Without being clear about it, they say: The strengthened senses should absorb more information than usual (which would probably not be wrong)."

"People who use this word," remarked CP, "probably mean a kind of spiritual, metaphysical experience."

"For sure. When they create such an aim in themself, a midpoint will form that will make them feel that way. Of course, this only happens in their brains.

Anyway", I continued, "the experiments of Libet and others (scientific writings by Benjamin Libet 1983, Keller and Heckhausen 1990, Haggard and Eimer 1999, Miller and Trevena 2002) clearly show that, before a person made a conscious decision, the brain does this decision has already been made. So, you cannot deny that the brain is deciding and not consciousness.

One particular difficulty was that in earlier times it could not be precisely defined: Consciousness was something that was not found in the brain but, as people said, controls one's actions. Because the belief in supernatural, in this case a 'consciousness-spirit being' was widespread."

"They took consciousness as a metaphysical spirit, similar to the spirit of God, without questioning it further."

I nodded. "And unfortunately, that is still the case today.

The fact that the brain decides has been clearly demonstrated by the experiments of Libet and other scientists.
The so-called "freedom of consciousness" has never been proven."

"But why do educated people still cling to their version that this decides everything?"

"It fits in well with their worldview and has always been considered a cognitive and decision-making authority. One was and is sure that the entire true world could be recognized with it.

In the past, the brain explained that the world was unique - to handle it well - and that it could be perceived and recognized by people with their consciousness. Of course, that lifted the human far beyond the animals. At the latest since the emergence of the theory of relativity and quantum mechanics and their experimental confirmation, this belief is over: The world is neither unique nor the same from every perspective.

What remains in many people is the idea of the consciousness that the decision is made, because, according to its logic, it recognizes everything. Of course, this logic excludes the brain - as a decision-maker.

But consciousness is just an important interface between the brain and the outside world," I explained. "Only with its senses - and it is an amplification of these - is it possible for the brain to receive specific information from the outside and of course also from the inside."

"So, if something is important, then the senses are reinforced and consciousness comes into play," repeated CP.

"Imagine that you have the aim of making an important decision, of choosing or pronouncing judgment on the basis of relevant facts, and you should do all of this in every single sequence with just your awareness, like many people accept.

Or let's take the language, it runs automatically. One has learned how to speak, articulate and so on. An experienced speaker, of course, does not focus on the individual points of the language, but the focus is on the topic at stake.

The speaking, the gestures, the facial expressions that one makes, all this has been learned in the course of life and is, if one speaks, expressed. Consciousness has nothing to do with it, unless you behave wrong, make mistakes, then it usually becomes active immediately and delivers appropriate information to the brain. This then attempts to bring about a correction or change in behaviour.

Imagine, you have to choose all your words only with your consciousness. For example, at a party. And now ask yourself what you are really aware of. That means: how to use your movements, how you speak, facial expressions, etc. "

"That's really impossible, you need the learned routines from the brain," CP agreed.

"Yes, the respective midpoints."

"You say only the relatively most important things come to your consciousness. But how is it when I am busy with an important topic and concentrate on it. Suddenly, something comes to my consciousness that has nothing to do with the current midpoint? "

"Well, the brain jumped from one midpoint to another because it took the attention or because the previous one might just go by itself and no longer need consciousness. Or the other midpoint seemed more important to the brain at the moment, because a question that had been in one for a long time could now be answered. This often happens with creative people. Maybe they just aroused interest in some topic.

By the way: It also occurs to me that when you've forgotten something that you just wanted, it can help sometimes to ask yourself: 'What was my aim just now?'"

"You mean you jumped to another midpoint, and is less shaped by the previous one?"

I nodded. "It's like priming*.

And in general, the following applies: A very strong concentration is only possible for a limited time, because from a certain point, due to physiological factors, it decreases. "

"And otherwise, you live without consciousness?" asked CP. "If everything works and no new facts are added?"

I smiled. "Most of the time, everything actually goes off automatically, the consciousness is almost in the standby state during this time, but is immediately active again when something important occurs. Usually, this is far less the case than you should think. In addition, the brain learns, and the new usually quickly becomes routine, so that the consciousness is then no longer needed in this intensity.

If you observe yourself, you will be able to confirm this. In everyday life, you don't usually come across

115

something exciting new or important events.

- So, attention has the task of being 'on the job' at the respective midpoints.

- The consciousness to concentrate, if necessary, in order to convey to the brain, the information that is considered to be very relevant."

"Consciousness always becomes active with intense attention when something is very important," CP repeated.

"Yes. Depending on what the attention is focused on, this gets a value that can shape or, in other words, structure man. This is the normal attention. If something is particularly important, then one speaks of a conscious recording.

Also, at the risk of repeating myself: the purpose is to provide this strong information to the aims in the brain so that they can immediately absorb them and respond accordingly. So, consciousness is always an enhancement of the senses. "

"So, attention and consciousness each deliver information to the brain?"

"Yes, the difference is in the different valence."

"Consciousness is not active that often."

"If you observe yourself, you will be able to confirm this. In everyday life you do not usually encounter something exciting new or important events.

But here one should differentiate: Adolescents and especially children have more consciousness than adults. Consciousness in the sense of increased perception. Because the world is still new and they are gathering their experiences. But that does not necessarily mean that its perception corresponds to the facts. (Because the aims in the brain guide the perception).

Conversely, it seems that the older you are, the less you usually integrate in yourself. Experience shows that neuronal plasticity is limited. However, this is less the case for areas that have interested people for life.

Many midpoints have become firmer over the years, but also more rigid, and unfortunately often exclude new things that seemingly do not suit them with the midpoint-mechanics.

In addition, it could be interesting: Until you are around 28 years old, the bottom-up works - the sustainable recording of information that is used to shape the value of the respective person. Then comes the bottom-down - acting with established information. (One acts from the value creation that has taken place.)
Incidentally: The content of this acquired information and values is, however, usually only marginally scientifically secured.

Consciousness awakens or generates midpoints because of important values in the brain when they are particularly touched. For example: survival, new orientation, social recognition.

Is it overwhelmed or bored, then one comes to dreams.

However, the moment you leave your habitual environment, for example, the attention or consciousness becomes more active. Because new facts or impressions are important to the brain to orient itself. Movements and pictures are preferably consciously perceived. "

"What mechanism may be behind this if you're stuck with a topic, even though you think you know the solution?" CP asked.

"It's a midpoint that blocks. For example, one has gotten bogged, and in this impasse the thoughts circle. The same mechanism works when one is ruled by anger*. Generally speaking, whenever there is a midpoint that severely restricts others. "

"That reminds me," CP said, "if you've slept on it, the solution often comes to mind the next day."

"That's because the blocking midpoint has lost value or dissolved in the meantime. We have found a distance. In sleep, amongst others the brain has the task to integrate the experiences of the day's events, to learn, and possibly to create a different view through restructuring. For this, the brain prefers to use the creativity that the midpoints of the day's events can not interfere with."

"You see things in a different light," thought CP.

"Yes, the attitude changes. In other words, the other midpoints associated with this topic have been re-evaluated or others have been added. Unless this dead-end midpoint acts in the same form. Then you have a complex, so to speak.

By the way: We all know that the brain can be mistaken when it comes to recognizing and especially feeling. Therefore, before you decide something important, you should sleep on it for a night. "
--- complexes ---

"Please explain 'complex' again."

"It's a midpoint, a neural network that is unable to adapt and offers strong resistance to attempts at change."

"Has it encapsulated himself?"

"Yes, in contrast to the midpoints, which can always be learned.

Or to the clusters. These are neural networks that carry out learned or innate processes and are adaptable - such as sucking the baby on the mother's breast, walking or tying shoes. "

A cluster is therefore a midpoint, which is responsible among other things for routines, such as movements, recurring actions, learned reactions. Can you give a graphic example? "CP asked.

"Well, about a tic - a short and uncontrollable motor contraction of individual muscles in the face - is a complex. By contrast, normal facial expressions are a cluster. "

"There are, as you said, many clusters in one - skills, learned procedures, behaviours, attitudes, etc.

Can one say: complex means encapsulated?"

"Yes, it surrounds himself with walls. His aim is to maintain certain attitudes, postures, reflexes under all circumstances, and to influence other midpoints with his peculiarity of maintaining what he has once learned in a particular situation.

There are also among others Life-complex, producer-complex, Complex to follow someone. These lie entirely in the depths of the human being. This is how he is born and they practically cannot be changed.

► **The life-complex is the drive to live as long as you can, regardless of the circumstances.**

► **The producer-complex is the mainspring to produce offspring, regardless of the environmental conditions.**

► **The Complex to follow someone is devotion to a person of importance or authority who has been given special skills and whom one trusts to the point of blindness.**

As with all complexes, there is a risk of not adapting to the changed circumstances. "

"That means," thought CP, "they are rigid and do not act like other midpoints that are flexible and play along in concert with the aims of the brain."

"Yes, they don't act like the healthy midpoints, and don't learn and thus disrupt the flexibility and adaptation of the brain. This is of course unfavourable. The outside world is constantly changing. The central point of life in general and the resulting requirement should be that man adapts to these changes.

That's usually the case. Complexities prevent this, as do prejudices*, delusions, stubbornness, intolerance*. And especially fanaticism or dogmatism. "

"This is quite common," commented CP.

--- worldview ---

"I have another question," he continued. "Apart from the obviously irrefutable fact that everything consists of substances that operate according to laws*: How can one explain that there are people who believe your view of the world is the only true one? "

"You can see that very clearly in extremists, fanatics, devout believers, people who are nailed up," I nodded.

"But also, the other 'normal' people have fixed midpoints. These are their anchors, their reference points, from which they act and evaluate the world.

Anyone who realizes that their perspective is just one of many is less in danger of being torn away from the ground by the abandonment of a midpoint.

Unfortunately, here as well, the midpoints act to diminish everything else that does not support them.

For clarification once again:

The world that we see is of course still there, even if we are no longer there. However, it would change according to the respective perception by other beings who are different from us.

Because there is no such thing as a world that is always the same.

What stays forever - no matter what perspective you look at it from - is that identical substances under identical conditions always show identical results.

Many people refuse to give up a midpoint, even if it dawns on them that it is harmful to themselves. Partly because they are afraid of losing their grip.

This fear is more justified for extremists and strict believers than for other people, because they are only made special from one or a few midpoints. This is how their world could actually fall apart.

The more midpoints in a person who can play flexibly and communicate with each other, the better it is."

"Because other midpoints can intercept the inner system?"

"Yes, especially if you have focused on not just a few midpoints in your life, but many."

"You mean, if you are not just focusing on your beliefs, your family, a loved

125

one you are fixated on, your job, your hobby, etc. you can be at risk through these midpoints if you are fully immersed in them are not seeing anything else in the long run?"

"I think so."

"So, you do not have to give up your special midpoints?" CP asked.

"You do not need that. But one thing to watch out for is that the midpoints you love will eventually get a place in one that guarantees that others will retain their value more or less. "

"Well, that a midpoint does not become a dominant ruler."

"Yes, that's important for inner harmony."

"That reminds me of complexes we just talked about."

"Midpoints that master everything are complexes."

"So, you should try to change or dissolve them," I suggested.

"That's usually difficult. If you have recognized a complex and tried to work on it, then this meets with considerable resistance. "

"What options are there?"

"You can divide the psyche of man, that is, the midpoints in the brain, into accessible and difficult to access.

If a complex interferes with healthy behaviour, and you cannot change it yourself, it is the job of a therapist, for example, to give that complex access to change or dissolve it.

The work of the brain is usually unconscious. It becomes aware when certain thresholds are exceeded. So, when something important is in the foreground, consciousness comes into action to provide information to the midpoints involved through more intense consciousness. "

"And this information does not take the encapsulated complex?"

"These can be very resistant to change - like many aims.

However, a complex does not necessarily have to be analysed down to the smallest detail, or become aware of it, so that it can be changed. If it is a learned behaviour, it is often enough to unlearn it again.

The method, such as the fear of crossing large squares, is to cross very small squares first, which can become larger if the client feels less anxious.

With others it makes more sense, as I said, to look for the reason (which always had an aim as the cause why it was formed). In this way one can possibly create an access if the consciousness stimulates a new midpoint that can bring about changes."

"You mean," concluded CP, "the one was learned and could be unlearned again. The other has formed at some point in a lifetime and could be worked through by rediscovering or raising consciousness."

"In all cases, it's about forming a new midpoint, which is increasingly reinforced by emotions and counterbalances the complex midpoint that narrows, oppresses or torments people. And who weakens or extinguishes this through the natural course of the midpoint mechanics."

"And what about the mind or the reason?"

"They can say umpteen times: 'It is nonsense what you do or think.' As long as you have not convinced the feeling, it will hardly be of any use.

--- Feelings ---

"How about the feelings when they become aware?" CP jumped to the next topic.

"Feelings are powerful controls in humans," I explained. "They arise among other things by achieving or not achieving aims.

Reaching the path strengthens the path that one had taken to reach the aim in a similar situation. If an aim is not achieved, negative feelings are triggered, which are intended to dissuade you from taking the same path in the future. At the same time, they more or less urge you to continue pursuing the aim.

Consciousness passes this information on to the brain's aims so that they can be processed by their networks. The stronger feelings for something, the more the human being gets in this midpoint. "

"Because this midpoint is reinforced by consciousness?"

"Yes, when we, for example, hear music.

Here the Qualia problem of the philosophers is often addressed.

'Qualia' means quality, quality is 'value'. The quality of a value results from the feelings that people feel (especially consciously). "

"Qualia means emotional value."

"Yes, people are sensitive to music because it creates feelings in them. The more beautiful these are, the more value they have for him. "

"That's how the value of music comes from the feelings you feel," said CP. "That's nothing new."

I nodded. "That these feelings are triggered by a midpoint is something new.

Many philosophers do not understand this, because the midpoint-mechanics are unknown to them. They say that while the brain can perceive all sorts of stimuli, it does not explain the enjoyment of the music we feel.

I say that this enjoyment comes from the midpoint in which I am when I listen to music. Of course, this network of neurons not only absorbs the stimuli, but also wholeheartedly arouses feelings that arise in connection with this music. "

"The more beautiful you feel music, the more beautiful feelings it develops," added CP.

"Yes, of course the reverse is also true: the worse the music, the less positive feelings will unfold."

"And if someone is completely unmusical?"

"Then he feels next to nothing in this respect."

"So, the extent to which a Qualia can develop depends on the people who receive it," CP concluded. The qualia are mutually determined by the mind and the consciousness: From one midpoint of the receiver, to the other by the quality of the sender."

I nodded again. "To feel holistic often means to feel a similarity*. This can be seen very well in the music: You can recognize a melody that has been stored in memory, even if it is played with other instruments. Unless the instruments do not hit the tone, that is the essence of this melody. "

"Why have so many philosophers struggled to grasp this simple mechanism for over 200 years?" Asked CP.

"Because they did not know about midpoint-mechanics, so they did not have that key to the brain, they thought of consciousness as something not ultimately comprehensible, and because feelings in their subjects were often just a minor matter. This applies especially to the followers of the philosopher Immanuel Kant, who portrayed the feelings as 'opponents of reason'.

Of course, feelings have a very high value for humans - not only in the negative, but of course in a positive sense. They are strong helpers of the aims - the midpoints. They control man and are not always unreasonable. What would a person be without feelings? "

"Philosophers can come to strange conclusions," CP shook his head.

I weakened. "What happened had to happen as it happened."

--- control ---

"Why is consciousness so important to many people?" He asked again.

"Because they often believe that they would decide everything with it. They need it for the feeling that they can determine absolutely freely. They don't want to realize that the brain's purposes have judged them.

They don't even want to be aware of that because they fear that they will

133

no longer have control over themselves."

"But do people actually have control over themselves? According to everything you have explained, the brain is infinitely diverse and decides holistically with the acute goals.

"Of course, you have more or less control, because the aims of the SELF are, as I have already explained, also in the psyche and play a part in the process.

The SELF can control areas of the psyche up to certain limit thresholds and, if necessary, influence them to a greater or lesser extent with its will. In other words, overcoming other aims in his psyche via the midpoint-mechanism.
But the stronger the feelings, the more difficult it becomes.
In general, the more the feelings have the power in the aims, the more difficult it is for the mind when differences arise.
This has to explain itself - not feelings! They run according to the laws within them, which can make it difficult for the mind to influence.

This will also have something to do with the fact that people have developed in the course of their evolution through feelings - the mind only much later.
Also because of this - and because it is much easier than trying to reason - the feeling is often preferred.

And: There are, of course, a number of midpoints that have a certain strength and cannot simply be ruled by the SELF, such as the life instinct.

So many people are subject to an exaggerated illusion of control."

"After all, one shouldn't forget: The more important a decision is, the more conscious it becomes," I repeated once more. "So, because people are aware of these brain decisions every time, they think they are making decisions with their consciousness.

In addition, until the 19th century, people knew little about the brain. That changed in the 20th and especially in the 21st century with the triumph of computers. This has created non-invasive methods such as:

EEG (electroencephalography),

MRI (magnetic resonance imaging),

fMRI (functional magnetic resonance imaging),

PET (positron emission tomography)

and CT (computed tomography).

These procedures allow insight into the brain, providing facts that were previously unknown.

But the old conceptions of consciousness that have been taught for thousands of years are still in people's minds today and are difficult to change. "

--- condemnation ---

"I have a question about criminal acts," CP said. "The judiciary assumes that humans are responsible for their actions.*."

"If someone commits an act, then he is in focus of the aim during this period, and it is usually not possible for the perpetrator to stop: the aim

136

structures people, it wants to be fulfilled."

"Can't consciousness experience the effects once the brain made the decision?"

"Then of course - but not from the point of view of the aims of the brain that currently prevail."

"And he can't watch himself? Can't he be aware of what he's doing? "

"At the moment of the crime, the midpoint of the criminal act is usually so strong that it suppresses everything else."

"It is really strange that while the brain, more precisely, the midpoint decides, people do not notice this and believe it came from consciousness - that is seen as the SELF with its 'free will'."

"This is exactly what the judges believe, because they assume, as you have rightly said, that consciousness decides everything and the will is free, and both could have prevented the act."

"But if the brain has made its decision, then the consciousness could use information to signal that this is wrong," CP tried again.

"This usually excludes the aim of the midpoint. And if so, this would only work if this information is perceived and accepted by the brain, which does not happen.

Because as I said: the perpetrator is in a focus. This mechanism controls him completely, even if only for a short time. In addition, the criminal act has set a certain process in motion that is not so easy to stop. "

"So, you couldn't express any criticism at that moment, because all other midpoints - which otherwise influence perception - hardly come into play," concluded CP.

"I agree. This possible resistance in one can hardly exist as long as one is in the midpoint of this decision, because it ensures that one practically does not perceive anything else. And, as I said, it sets everything else in value to almost zero. After that you often become aware of what you have done. But then of course you can no longer correct it. "

--- Freedom / Determinism ---

For a moment it was quiet between us. Then CP continued, "Can one say: Everyone knows he has consciousness, but hardly anyone has been able to define it yet?"

I nodded. "Although this is actually easy if you accept the midpoint-mechanics and are not totally absorbed by your fixed ideas: **Consciousness is intensive perception with your senses, holistically or in detail.**

Consciousness is also about the issue of man's spiritual freedom. If it turns out that everything runs according to substances and laws*, then everything would be predetermined, then man would have quasi no freedom and the free will would not be there then - from the legal and philosophical point of view."

"And - is that right?" asked CP.

"The will is of course still there and plays an important role in the life of

139

man. Will means to form a particularly strong aims for the SELF, which is also in the brain.

And human freedom would continue - because he does not know everything. And who does not know everything, is forced to make decisions. **This ignorance is his freedom**, which man will not lose because he can never know everything.

But consciousness and **free will** in the previous sense would have to be given up.

And in the end, the fact is that everything is made up of substances that run according to laws and, as a result, everything is predetermined. "

"You do not mean the freedom that comes from nowhere, but the freedom of the possibilities one has. Is that ultimately freedom?" asked CP.

"It's a quasi-freedom," I answered. It is definitely a mistake to believe that there is a freedom that comes from nothing or an incomprehensible mind."

One more remark on the "spirit": A spirit, in the sense of an immaterial being, which our ancestors had felt internally and then projected outwards, because the functions of the brain - also with regard to the midpoint mechanics - were completely unknown to them only exist in humans. Everything else is projections that have no substance whatsoever in reality.

The spirits in one self are the midpoints.

They can arise and fade, in the respective context with regard to a certain value they more or less play along and shape people.

Midpoints have the ability to suddenly show people a world that is completely different from what they are used to.

--- SELF – IT - SUPEREGO ---

CP thought about it and then said: "There are also a lot of theories about what happens psychologically in people."

"You could say so. I would like to give an example: **An attempt was made to divide the psyche (that is, the totality of aims and their midpoints in humans**, which work via neuronal networks. For example, into SELF, It, Super-SELF, how Sigmund Freud did it.

He wrote: "The psychoanalytic" drive "is the basis of all expressions of life - regardless of the differentiated level."

If he had said aims instead of instinct, he would have come very close to the truth. Urges also play their part, of course, but are ultimately just aims. And reducing everything to urges does not lead to the reality of the psyche.

So, this does not go to the core of reality.

This is that the entire brain (which also includes the so-called abdominal brain) is a dynamic system in which the midpoints all communicate with one another more or less - and depending on the respective topic.

If one divides the psyche with three terms (self, ego, super-ego) and understands these as separate areas, it is problematic as an explanation of the soul and useless for the diagnosis of the complicated psychic processes.

Each individual component of these terms has not only developed from aims into a neural network that is located in the brain, but also correlates, mostly unconsciously, with others.

So, there are not three major areas in the psyche, but a multitude of aims:

In every living being there is a spectrum of aims that relate, detach, connect with one another, form groups that act together, overlap, struggle for supremacy and arrange themselves in a sometimes-alternating hierarchy. Aims are added, others change or erase. Every aim has or creates its opponent when other aims are touched by it and run the risk of being impaired. And every action takes place through a bundle of aims that develop structures, compromise, strengthen or weaken. Many aims change in the course of life, except for the very deep ones, e.g., the life instinct. As a rule, this always remains, even if you are very old.

In this living space the behaviours are formed: actions, planning, acting, etc., the drive of instincts, and the feelings of conscience.

These are not delimited, but are subject, among other things, to the laws of midpoint-mechanics.

►In this example, the 'ego' should be the consciousness that intervenes regulatively in the processes of the psyche.

In addition, it has the task of observing social norms, values, obedience and morality.
One can say that the consciousness only supplies the brain with information that it has received through intensive perception and that is then more or less processed by the respective midpoints - which was not known earlier. The ego is represented with its aims and midpoints in the brain and these can possibly intervene in the processes of the psyche (if it allows it) to regulate.

And as I said: **Consciousness is not the Self.**

> ►The 'it' in this case is intended to represent the unconscious, whose content are the instincts, needs and affects.

It can be said that what one is unconscious of involves much more than these three areas, namely, among other things, procedures, communication attitudes, adaptation to the respective environment, etc.

It is also not the case that this must necessarily remain unconscious, but all these actions become conscious when they exceed a certain threshold value.

> ►Finally, the 'super-ego' represents in the model the morality, the social norms and the conscience, which is supposed to intervene in the processes of the id, that is to say the impulses, needs, affects.

One can say that morality is stored in aims, as well as social norms, etc. Conscience is a feeling that is triggered by judgments of good or evil that are also generated by aims. "

"Pangs of conscience therefore arises when one has not behaved according to the moral ideas that have formed in one," concluded CP.

I nodded. "And if, for example, you committed an act that you believe you are guilty of."

"Why were such theories born?" asked CP. "They really don't depict the complicated processes in the brain."

"At that time, one did not know otherwise, theories of the time, which, like these, fell on fertile ground, because here the role of the unconscious was presented more clearly for the first time.

Until then, one had more or less thought that one dominates himself only with his consciousness. This theory was something new, the time was right and it was very simple.

The time was also ripe, because at that time the prudery was driven to the extreme, which led to sexual neurosis. That was a strong focus of this theory building.

Such theories can last a long time - like habits. And have been defended for a long time.

Freud pointed out that people are not always masters of their own houses - because unconscious currents can take control.

But with his division of the psyche into three separate areas, he unfortunately did not hit the facts.

Because the psyche arises from aims that form neural networks (midpoints) in order to reach it. Countless of these evolve in order to be able to survive and adapt in the world.

All are more or less connected with each other and act particularly depending on the current aims.

And one more word about the dreams:

What one dreams is not the essential; but how you yourself interpret your dreams.

Because then, through the research in your deeper SELF, aims are touched that otherwise can only, unconsciously, play along in the great concert of the psyche. Because, as a rule, they cannot be perceived by the midpoints during wakefulness for a wide variety of reasons.

For example:

In contrast to being awake, where aims of adaptation with the cerebrum dominate, dreams are about topics of the respective living being that are no longer influenced by the midpoints. The cerebrum, among other things, does not play a role here because it has largely been shut down. This is how the fantasies of dreams are perceived as reality.

Sleep is about recovery from wakefulness, in which one can constantly be brought back from the midpoint into structures.

In the dream it is about the continued working of the senses, which are now directed inwards. Since a number of functions of the brain have been shut down, they show topics and processes that are not geared towards a final result - like the aims (although here, too, only substances run according to laws).

You shouldn't take your dreams so seriously. They are surreal stimuli, scenes or stories that arise through associations, similarities, etc. Overall, however, they have little to do with reality.

How to perceive the world
(Definition and explanation)

One can look at the world as a fixed entity that is the same from every point of view.
This is called outside-in theory.

However, one can also see the world in such a way that different creatures see it differently in terms of their aims.
This is what I call the

inside-out theory.

There, as here, the sensors
receive stimuli from the
outside world. A few
impulses are enough to get
an idea.

In contrast to the outside-
in theory, however, the
world is created by the
respective living beings
according to their goals:
The sensors send the
recorded information to the
neural networks. If it is
determined there that the
world they perceive differs
from that stored in the
midpoints, they may process
their view of the world.
This process can be followed
immediately:

The world that living
beings, including humans,
perceive is one that results
from **their aims that neural
networks have built up**.
(Just as after conception
the body builds itself
according to inherited aims,
so does the psyche: **these
aims create neural networks**
in order to be reached.)

According to these, the
sensors see the world. As
soon as the inner world
differs from the outer
world, the neural networks
may change their structures.

This is how man perceives
the world according to his
psychic aims.

‼ The world that shows itself to us is of course there first, but what people absorb from it is decided by the brain according to its aims. ‼

Even if you want to record everything that is around you, it always remains a matter of the limits of our senses and brain.

Wikipedia (definition): In living beings, perception is the process and the subjective result of information acquisition (reception) and processing of stimuli from the environment and from the body. This happens through unconscious (and sometimes conscious in humans) filtering and merging of partial information into subjectively meaningful overall impressions. These are also called precepts and are continuously compared with stored ideas (constructs and schemes).

> ▶ According to this definition, there would be the world first, which is created by filtering and merging partial information into

153

subjectively meaningful overall impressions in living beings.

This raises the question: According to which directives are the filtering and merging of partial information carried out?

The answer could only be: Through the aims in the brain, which are focused by means of the sensors, which are focused by its values (aims) (i.e. where the attention should be directed).

▶ So, I think it's the other way around: that first the brain (the midpoints) has an approximate expectation about the world according to its aims. Then this is perceived by the senses selected in this way. Once this is done, inequalities in these two worlds (expectation and fact) are corrected by the brain in

milliseconds when it feels right according to its aims.

First of all, you always see the world according to your habits, expectations, and ideas that are stored in your brain about aims. If it recognizes (because it is valuable) that it deviates from it, then the perception is adjusted accordingly. Aims learn or form a new – again initially according to the aims that one has inherited or learned, because only through them can one originally perceive the world.

There is no world as it actually and always is, but only one from the perspective of the respective observer.

Therefore, we do not see the world as it appears to be in front of us (that is, the same for everyone), but one that the brain shows us based on its aims.

Since every person has their own characteristic aims, they also see their own world, to which they react individually.

(By the way, since each species has its specific goals, the world sees them similarly).

Again: People can only perceive the world from the perspective of the respective observer.

For clarification:

The world that we see is of course still there, even if we are no longer there. However, it would change according to the respective perception by other beings who are different from us.

Because there is no such thing as a world that is always the same.

What stays forever - no matter what perspective you look at it from - is that <u>identical substances under identical conditions always show identical results.</u>

Summarized:

> Human beings see the world from their point of view. This results from the aims of the respective person. Namely from his currently active ones or especially from those currently additionally stimulated.

> ▶ The active aims shape the world into a structure that is needed to achieve them.

> ▶ Depending on the value of the stimuli that are now activated, further aims are awakened, which additionally structure the view.

> ▶ So, there is ultimately no identical world that everyone sees the same, but many different, from the point of view of the respective aims.

And: intellect means to perceive something precisely, i.e. to understand it. You can only grasp what you have a system for.

(If one encounters something absolutely new, then of course one can also take in and grasp it - but, as I said, only according to one's predispositions aims). In this way, the new from the environment and inner field of the human being, from the brain, becomes his predispositions adjusted accordingly.

So, you absorb the world first through the aims in yourself and then with the aligned senses – in that order.

The senses are constantly confronted with unfiltered stimuli (approx. 11 million bits per second), but they do not simply represent the world in front of us 1:1, but the brain selects them with its aims, which align the senses in such a way that they only perceive the information that fits the aims of the brain because it is important.

These million bits are not there to depict the environment precisely for us, but to compare the structures that arise after selection through our aims with those stored in the brain and, if necessary, to correct them by learning (changing synapses).

In general, then, man has his hereditary world in the head brain, the autonomic nervous system (plus the somatic nervous system) and the abdominal brain (enteric nervous system), along with those who have experiences and learning were built in him.

This is the reason why we each perceive the world differently and possibly wrongly; because we weren't in the right midpoints. (Wrong in relation hung that we have disadvantages, e.g., not respond appropriately.)

And since the selection by the aims also influences the storage of experiences in the brain, this can lead to incorrect information.

A little excursion to objectivity:

How do animals, bacteria and viruses perceive the world?

And who sees the world more correctly?

Of course, people will say: the world ultimately looks the way we see it.

Anyone who says you can only see the world from a human perspective is definitely **right**.

Anyone who believes that this is being said about a basic world that is eternal and unchangeable is certainly **wrong**.

Because the world is basically **not** in an eternally identical state (because processes are constantly taking place on all levels).

A little incentive to think:

What should the brain also perceive when you say you see it for what it is?

The answer is only possible in relation to aims that reside in oneself - in the brain.

And: people's perception is limited. As for hearing and seeing with the respective bandwidth. Or e.g., the inability to perceive radioactivity, magnetism, ultrasound, etc.

There is no world that is the same and unchangeable from every perspective.

Summarized:

Viewed from living beings, the world is subjective.

Recorded by an apparatus - regardless of the perspective - it is always objective.

But this does not mean: forever fixed and immutable, because the world is constantly changing.

Only the laws according to which substances move are eternal.

And all perspectives of the macro- or micro world result in the sentences:
- **Identical substances under identical circumstances always give identical results.**

**• The reason for this is that everything is subject to unchangeable laws.
• If you change substances or circumstances, then other laws also appear.**

If you turn 180 degrees in a strange environment, it takes milliseconds before you consciously perceive what is in front of you.

This attaches to the brain: First, the general perception occurs according to its expectations. (If there are no specific ones, it looks for similarities). Depending on the extent to which this does not match what is in front of you, it is corrected if it is relevant.

The aim of orientation requires data from the senses to clarify whether and to what extent the world shown by the brain may deviate from reality in order to be able to adapt. This takes milliseconds. (The aim of orientation is a central aim in living beings).

Recognition also takes place through aims; one recognizes what was stored in the brain. This is also where the reason for confusion can be found (because the brain searches for similarities).

The selected stimuli may change existing neuronal networks in the brain or generate new ones if aims (midpoints) in the psyche consider this to be important. If the stimuli show more or less strong differences from what has been stored up to now, it is adjusted.

By means of the senses, which send information to the brain via attention, this is always up to date - if the aims of perception are not restricted too much by certain (rigid) midpoints.

Without new information from the senses, the brain is virtually blind - and only acts according to the previous information it had stored - as happens in a dream.

First you see the world that you last saved in yourself. If the senses recognize this differently, the storage changes - if the brain decides, this is important.

> E.g., when a landscape that has been seen fleetingly but assessed as irrelevant is seen by the senses. (The brain stays with its vision). <

> It is different when, for example, you wake up from sleep and the world saved before going to bed has changed. At first you see - expected - the world after the routine storage. But if the senses send other stimuli, then the brain will include them in its vision, because it is usually important in order to be able to deal with the immediate world. The evaluation and any change take place very quickly (as I said: in milliseconds). <

> This is also how it happens in dreams: the senses, which are directed inward due to sleep, take the stimuli of the dream world as facts that the brain - and consequently we - take as reality due to its changed structure during sleep. <

Regarding knowledge, individual things are not important. It all depends on the aim. If this is to look at details, only then will these be particularly perceived. But when it comes to saving the overall impression, then you perceive it as a whole.

The perception of music can serve as an example: You perceive the whole and not the individual instruments, because that is not the aim. (The whole thing is to perceive the feeling of music). The perception of individual devices would cloud the perception, because it could lead to other central points and be distracted.

This is exactly how you absorb everything in daily life from your goals. And that's how you see the world.

If something is no longer correct (e.g., something dangerous appears) then a target is activated in order to perceive it specifically. This suddenly puts you in a different focus. This is also recorded holistically and creates a different pattern in the brain.

Again: How and with what a room is filled is initially not important as long as one is aiming to perceive this room. Only when you look more closely through other aims do they gain value.

Conclusion: the brain always absorbs holistically. The stimulated aims can change the topics quickly.

Midpoint-mechanics

(Conversation about)

The midpoint-mechanics is the key to the psyche.

CP and I went for a walk around the lake Alster in Hamburg.

"Why do aims in your scriptures play such a central role?" *CP* wanted to know.

"Well, because they structure everything, put it in a shape: **Everything has the aim to form a structure according to the laws.**

Let's take the human being: **The midpoint is the shape that makes an aim out of a person.**

As a general knitting pattern, the example of how to learn to ride a bike:

167

In the beginning there is the aim. This creates a neural network in the brain to reach it.

Balance, muscles, tendons, posture, mental processes, etc. are developed as sub-goals in the required form, coordinated with one another and temporarily stored.

So gradually the skills are improved; you learn from your mistakes.

This is all done by the neural networks formed by the aim of cycling and then further evolving to expand body-psyche coordination and fine-tune adjustments.

The network at the beginning (the focus of cycling) has now become far-reaching interdependencies. Which, when the respective sub-goals have been achieved, are stored permanently and become an automatic behaviour that is activated when you get back on the bike.

While everything in the universe is shaped by aims that are 'no matter' to the implications of their intended structure, the aim of conservation is added to living beings. These conservation aims are formed in the brain by networks of neurons, which are connected via synapses and which, as I said, I call 'midpoints'.

Depending on the species and individual, the living beings are designed by them.

So, midpoints are made up of neurons distributed far the brain, forming a network that serves to create attitudes, actions, ideas, feelings, and so on. Each midpoint it's an aim that allows for everything that suits to achieve it, paying little or no attention to anything else."

It is very rare for only one midpoint to act; mostly, various are included that are suitable to achieve the goal. "

"Then the midpoint is a key to understanding human beings?"

"Yes - of all living beings. To reach an aim, you have to go one way. If you want to express 'way' more broadly, then you can say: you need a structure. And indeed, the way in the environment must be structured and of course the person who wants to achieve this aim. Everything that could contribute to this structure and is tangible at the moment is taken into account by the aim - everything else remains unused.

For example, if you focus heavily on reaching an aim, you will realize afterwards that he has not noticed anything else. Only what suited his purpose.

One comes closer to oneself each time one recognizes in which midpoint one was."

"I understood it that way," *CP* summarized: "A midpoint wants to be realized. This requires a specific structure. This is created from what is relevant, everything else is disregarded. Should something be disturbing, it is reduced in value, so it can make people much less".

I nodded. "This lowering of the other values does not happen willingly, but mechanically. It is a legal process, that's why I called it 'midpoint-mechanics'."

"It is not deliberately suppressed, but it happens automatically through the midpoint?"

"An example: On March 24, 2015, a pilot in a passenger plane flew into suicide. He steered the plane against a huge rock. He tore all 150 inmates to death.

What happened in the head of this person?"

"He has supplanted everything else," *CP* concluded.

"Imagine that you're focusing your attention on something you do not want to admit. This makes this something stronger because you are dealing with it (you are so in the midpoint of it, you are shaped by it). With repression, you get exactly the opposite of what you want, to put something aside. "

"But it is also said, 'One displaces something when something unconsciously continues to act.'"

"That is also incorrect in the true sense of the word. It is reduced in value from other midpoints so that it is no longer perceived, but can continue to work in the unconscious. – However, not if a current midpoint is very strong.

The answer to what was going on in the co-pilot's head is the midpoint-mechanics: The aim is to take his own life, sat all other midpoints worth reduced or zero - the impending impact of the mountains, the 150 people who were on board and had to die with him, their relatives who suffered the loss, etc.

On the one hand, it's frightening what midpoints can do, such as the incredible atrocities of the Nazi regime or inhumane acts that virtually all nations have perpetrated. "

"Or what individual people did to others," added *CP*.

"Yes. On the other hand, it's nice what midpoints can do. For example, the love to enter for humans or other living beings.

By the way: This also explains the essence of mediation: Here, a midpoint is formed, which becomes stronger with the time and the intensity and amount of the exercises and lowers all other midpoints in value.

As a rule, of course, there is not only one midpoint in the psyche, but many who complement each other, inhibit or only partially play along. They can act together, form mega-nets (clusters), for example, to ensure repetitive processes, integrate into new ones, find themselves together for specific actions.

As adaptation is a central theme for life, new midpoints are always forming.

Here's an example of how midpoints work: People like to argue about whether humans can be altruistic. Surely, he can, because: If he is in the midpoint of helping others, then the midpoints of selfishness, which are actually strong aims in humans, can be eliminated.

However, in the strict sense, there is no selflessness because the aim is to satisfy one's own feelings. "

"What can one do to avoid a midpoint, not to be a slave?"

"Beat him with his own weapons: choose another midpoint or create something new."

"How do you best achieve an aim?"

"By reinforcing the midpoint: paying attention only to what is important to the aim.

If that is not enough, then a new target can be formed that includes more neuron groups, which are automatically selected for how well they might contribute to the solution.

Again, you can see the selection principle of the midpoint.

In addition, similarities in other areas are searched for each aim. Whether there is experience, or by logic, such as the exclusion process, whether solutions are suitable for the problem. And rejects all offered 'solutions' that are illogical in the experience, not fit to achieve this aim or nothing similar to the one to a similarity Theme in common. "

"So, aims are the mainsprings?"

"As often as you investigate, you will always meet aims that have driven, structured the human being.

They can seriously change our perception: through the midpoint-mechanics.

Imagine a tremendous amount of aims that are interconnected. "

"You mean the brain."

"Yes, the neurons that are in contact with each other through the synapses. There are about 100 billion neurons and 100 trillion synapses in the brain. Neurons form networks to perform certain functions.

Everything in the brain runs according to laws. The brain creates the midpoints and these structures the human. "

We sat down on a bench and watched the sailboats cruising the Alster. It was a wonderful day.

> "I once wrote a conversation between Peter, a friend of mine, and Phil Osof, which I would like to reproduce here:"

"The midpoint means the world that is created to reach an aim," explained Phil Osof.

"An aim creates a world?"

"To achieve an aim, you need a structure. The midpoint is designed and is this structure. He evaluates the world and the people and puts together what is useful for achieving the aim. Everything else is more or less shielded."

"You think the midpoint is the facts that are interesting for the aim? And brings the people and the world in the appropriate form? "Peter hooked.

"The midpoint is the shape that makes an aim of a human.

He structures the perception of the outer world and of oneself. He chooses what he finds and thinks it has value for the aim. He gives shape to the world. "

"That really sounds like," Peter noticed, "as if through the midpoint a new world would emerge."

"That's right," Phil Osof nodded. "He's redesigning. This can go so far that you cannot see things as they were, because they are totally re-evaluated.

The midpoint can be like a sorcerer, changing everything with lightning speed. This is how a new world is created. This gives rise to freedom, meaning that one does not perceive much, or only perceives it marginally. At the same time, however, one is also trapped in the midpoint and no longer sees many things. It only comes to the fore, which is important. Everything else goes by, so to speak, suddenly has no value. "

"So, is the midpoint at the same time freedom and prison?" Peter wondered.

"That's the way to express it."

So, "midpoint" is what you call the perceptual world of living beings?" "he wanted to know.

"Yes, the world- and the self-perception. What and how creatures perceive depends on their aims, or in other words: we (our brains) do not simply model the world in ourselves, but create a world of perception based on our aims and the particular spectrum of our senses. The amount of information that comes from the world, but that we ultimately shape ourselves from our human perspective and can only capture within our intake corridors, must be selected. This will get the midpoints. They choose what fits the aims."

"I remember once saying, 'Everything is aligned with aims.'"

Osof nodded again. "Living beings are controlled exclusively by aims. There is nothing that does not originate in it. "

One more question came to Peters mind: "But is not the world actually what it is? How can she be so different and suddenly different?"

"When the aims change, the substances change. Because different substances are needed for each goal. And when they change, the world also changes because it is composed of substances. "

"From the human point of view," I interjected.

"Yes. But ultimately, what we see is always from the point of view of human beings."

"Then there is really no 'world in itself'?", I was curious.

"Yes - of course, the objective world can be depicted using photography, for example, because the subjective influences are not present here at first.

Beyond that, however, there are only views of it from the living beings. Every living entity sees her differently, from what is important to him. And this view shapes his world and himself.

The world is not a rigid entity, but a 'something' that can be seen infinitely varied by the living beings. And there are as many worlds as there are living things "

"That would mean that we ourselves make the world that we see through our aims."

"It is exactly like that".

"You say that a camera can image the world objectively?"

"Yes, depending on the setting (distance, resolution, special perspectives). However, the camera can only take a snapshot with it.

By the way: Without midpoints there would be no demarcation, without them no structures - and of course no life, because no figures could form in the world. The midpoints are the central factor of life. "

"Still," I shook my head, "I think the world is what it is, and we need to adapt, so shape it."

"Of course," Osof replied.

"But is not that a contradiction?" Peter wondered. "What do you think makes the world or us the world?"

"First of all, our brain shapes the world according to its aims - compares them with what it has holistically stored. When differences arise that it sees with its (enhanced) senses (and these differences have a certain value), then it learns.

Peter considered. "So, we see them according to our values (aims). And since everyone has their own individual aims, those of their group, their country and those of the respective community of values, this is how they see the world. "

"Exactly," nodded Osof.

‼ The world that shows itself to us is there first.

But what a person sees or perceives from this, the brain decides according to its aims.‼

Max Wertheimer: "There are connections in which not everything that happens as a whole derives from the way in which the individual pieces are composed, but conversely, where - in a pertinent case - what happens in a part of this whole, determined by internal structural laws of this his whole ".

When differences occur (and they have a certain value), the midpoints learn.

So, it can also absorb something totally new, if e.g., the aim of life is threatened."

"And we always only see the world that selects our aims, put together?"

"Yes," nodded Phil Osof, "that's how we make the world, we can only see it from a human perspective."

"That was an exhaustive information," *CP* thanked. "How did Phil Osof get to the mechanics of the midpoints?"

"Well, you can only come to that if you realize that everything is designed according to aims. And aims need certain structures in order to be achieved. Everything that could not contribute is ignored.

An example: A question arises on a complex topic. You find an answer. As a result, you usually no longer include all the factors that could be considered for this question, but only those factors that support the answer you have decided on."

"Does that mean that the midpoint changes due to the determination?"

"Yes, first you were in the midpoint, which takes into account all the essential facts, then only those who supported your own opinion were seen."

"If you don't get the answer right, it would be a threat to the right answer," CP concluded.

"Exactly, all other essential factors are suddenly no longer taken into account."

"These are really interesting examples of how midpoint mechanics work," CP concluded thoughtfully.

Epilogue

Let me say a few more basic words about the relationship between my (potential) readers and me:

People are guided by aims. These can and are influenced by the midpoint-mechanics. Also, in such a way that what speaks against them is perceived less or not at all.

As a rule, you don't notice anything about these processes because they are part of the routine that the brain carries out every day.

This influence also applies to a relatively large part of my representations regarding the perception by the readers.

For most of them, these are probably descriptions that don't match their image of humanity that they have within them.

That is unfortunate.

But I'm not interested in serving such expectations, but in writing what I've learned through my investigations.

Such as for example the issue of descendants, which plays a major role for all living beings.

I would like to repeat a Conversation:

"Why are children actually born?" Justin received me.

He was 24 years old, studied computer science and mathematics, was inquisitive with a quick wit and the son of rich parents who allowed him to grow up in a liberal and non-denominational way.

We met regularly in a small bistro.

"How did you come up with this question?"

"I once heard the expression, 'They gave a new born a gift of life.' I don't understand that."

"Because is has a meaning of a gift?"

"The term seems inappropriate to me."

"You mean the producers gave themselves the gift?"

"Yes, because her feelings drove them to it. If the child had not been born, it would have been spared the whole range of negative and positive experiences.

And – I heard from a 13-year-old whose serious cancer illness would only let him live a few months: 'I am grateful that I was allowed to live.'"

"Well, yes," I nodded, "at the very beginning of every new life, a chain of feelings is activated that strives for life. So, as soon as you're conceived, you're in the grip of life. It only let's go of you when you die.

Life is not primarily about knowledge. But to generate the midpoints of 'survival and offspring'."

"You mean, once you're conceived, you're in the grip of life. It only let's go of you when you are death."

I nodded again. "Procreation is about feelings: To create the Midpoint of progeny."

Justin continued, "So why do humans produce children in the first place? Although they should know that by doing so, they are begetting death. Because everyone has to die sometime.

But mainly to satisfy her feelings, as you say. Because the desire to have children can be incredibly strong.

I can understand it with animals; They cannot anticipate this process - people can.

It's incredible what people can do to have a child."

"Like you said, this is what feelings push you to do. That way it's not seen as something negative," I said. "And – just ask the children if they like to live and aren't happy that they were born."

"As you just pointed out, they will of course say 'yes'," he replied. "Because they are at the midpoint of the life instinct.

Life may still offer such horrible events as wars, natural disasters, devilish diseases, times of absolute need and the most terrible horror. Everything is repressed after a short time. Attention diverges and children keep being born.

This is how Justin explained that the midpoints in people when it came to be getting children made sure that death and suffering did not enter their consciousness at the time of procreation. The midpoints here were: sexuality, continuation of one's own sex, nursing instinct, the desire to realize one's ideas.

"You mean, having children is a self-serving for people?"

"Yes. That's how I see it. People care about their own interests and feelings."

Although I thought I knew the answer, I asked:

"Who would benefit if no more children were born?"

"The unborn. It would save them suffering and death."

"Who would possibly beget no more children through this insight?"

"People who can see through the urge for offspring's and have the strength to draw conclusions from it."

"If everyone thinks like that, wouldn't humanity die out?"

"You know it's impossible. The midpoint of life instinct is much too strong for that.

It occurs to me," Justin continued thoughtfully, "that there have always been people, especially from the religious camp, who wanted to "redeem" mankind.

In history, of course, no one has managed to do this, because that would probably only be possible by renouncing offspring.

For as long as life is born, there will be death and suffering."

"So, an 'eternal life' would not be an aim worth striving for?"

"No."

He looked thoughtfully out of the window.

"I have often asked myself the question: where does humanity want to go, what does it actually want to achieve?

A state of peace, freedom, harmony, salvation?

If you think consistently and go through life with open eyes, you will see that this is impossible in the long run.

History is characterized by self-interest - of the individual, of the groups, of the peoples. This is human nature. Certainly, there have been many attempts to bring people onto the path of salvation. But all of these attempts ended in failure in the end."

"If this view were to become known and conscious, could not many people, especially women, get into a painful conflict, for example with regard to their caregiving instinct, which they could not live out without children?"

"Yes. They have a choice to submit to the feelings created by evolution or to follow the simple insight I outlined.

But renouncing children will certainly not occur because, as I said, the focus of the drive to live is overpowering.

As a rule, people cannot act against their feelings here. And man don't want it too.

Seen in this way, living beings are also slaves to their aims."

"But doesn't everyone ultimately have to decide for themselves whether they want to father children, or not?" I asked.

"Of course," Justin replied. "I just wanted to make people aware of the problem and possible consequences.

Everyone should act according to their inner values. And here, as with all living beings, the offspring has a particularly high value."

Well, I thought, that was Justin's opinion. A wholly unusual view, though, which I had never heard from anyone else before.

On the way home, I reviewed the conversation and sent Justin this message:

After the origin of all life billions of years ago, the goal of surviving and later creating offspring was burned in and was transferred to all creatures that came into existence afterwards - including humans.

So, the purpose (goal) of life is to live and produce offspring. As I said, both are also deeply rooted in people – in their original structures.

I think the reason could have been: After life arose, creatures had to protect themselves from competition, among other things, if they wanted to survive. This worked best if you produced as many similar creatures as possible and then had them around. This is how the 'idea' of growth came about, and it stuck.

Finally, a word about the blindness of leaders

Ultimately, this affects everyone, because everyone sees themselves as the one who determines their fate with their free will.

This of course (via the midpoint mechanic) disables the view of himself - i.e. what is actually going on inside him. Namely: That it is shaped by goals that form neural networks in order to be achieved.

And since the leaders are vehemently sure of themselves, they are particularly blind to it.

Other books by me:

- Blindness of the wise
- Blindheit der Klugen
- Mittelpunkt der Psyche
- Midpoint of the psyche
- Die Entzauberung des Bewusstseins (geänderte Auflage)
- The disenchantment of consciousness
- Was Gläubige wissen sollten
- What Believers Should Know
- Die Nicht-Entstehung des Universums
- The non-creation of the universe
- Wutgefühle: (Wie Gefühle entstanden und den Menschen bewegen)
- Feelings of anger: (How feelings arose and move people)
- Die Welt ohne Metaphysik (Eine klare Sicht auf den Menschen und die Welt)
- 3 Gründe: Psychologische Grundlagen des Menschen ••• Physikalische Grundlagen der Welt ••• Betrachtungen des Glaubens
- 3 Basics of human beings